Greet the new year with this wintry snowflake doily. Its star quality has timeless appeal.

▰▰▰▱ INTERMEDIATE

Shown on page 1.

Finished Size: 12¼" (31 cm) diameter

MATERIALS
Bedspread Weight Cotton Thread (size 10)
[284 yards (260 meters) per ball]: One ball
Steel crochet hook, size 6 (1.8 mm) **or** size
needed for gauge

GAUGE SWATCH: 1⅞" (4.75 cm) diameter
Work same as Doily through Rnd 4.

STITCH GUIDE

3-DC CLUSTER (uses one sp)
★ YO, insert hook in sp indicated, YO and pull up a loop, YO and draw through 2 loops on hook; repeat from ★ 2 times **more**, YO and draw through all 4 loops on hook.

4-TR CLUSTER (uses one sp)
★ YO twice, insert hook in sp indicated, YO and pull up a loop, (YO and draw through 2 loops on hook) twice; repeat from ★ 3 times **more**, YO and draw through all 5 loops on hook.

DOILY
Ch 8; join with slip st to form a ring.

Rnd 1 (Right side)**:** Ch 3 **(counts as first dc, now and throughout)**, dc in ring, ch 2, (2 dc in ring, ch 2) 5 times; join with slip st to first dc: 12 dc and 6 ch-2 sps.

Rnd 2: Ch 3, dc in sp **before** next dc **(Fig. 13, page 39)**, dc in next dc, ch 2, ★ dc in next dc and in sp **before** next dc, dc in next dc, ch 2; repeat from ★ around; join with slip st to first dc: 18 dc and 6 ch-2 sps.

Rnd 3: Ch 3, 2 dc in same st, skip next dc, 3 dc in next dc, ch 2, ★ 3 dc in next dc, skip next dc, 3 dc in next dc, ch 2; repeat from ★ around; join with slip st to first dc: 36 dc and 6 ch-2 sps.

Rnd 4: Ch 3, 2 dc in same st, skip next 2 dc, 3 dc in sp **before** next dc, skip next 2 dc, 3 dc in next dc, ch 2, ★ 3 dc in next dc, skip next 2 dc, 3 dc in sp **before** next dc, skip next 2 dc, 3 dc in next dc, ch 2; repeat from ★ around; join with slip st to first dc: 54 dc and 6 ch-2 sps.

Rnd 5: Ch 3, 2 dc in same st, skip next 2 dc, 3 dc in sp **before** next dc, skip next 3 dc, 3 dc in sp **before** next dc, skip next 2 dc, 3 dc in next dc, ch 2, ★ 3 dc in next dc, skip next 2 dc, 3 dc in sp **before** next dc, skip next 3 dc, 3 dc in sp **before** next dc, skip next 2 dc, 3 dc in next dc, ch 2; repeat from ★ around; join with slip st to first dc: 72 dc and 6 ch-2 sps.

Rnd 6: Ch 3, 2 dc in same st, ★ † skip next 2 dc, 3 dc in sp **before** next dc, ch 2, skip next 3 dc, dc in sp **before** next dc, ch 2, skip next 3 dc, 3 dc in sp **before** next dc, skip next 2 dc, 3 dc in next dc, ch 2 †, 3 dc in next dc; repeat from ★ 4 times **more**, then repeat from † to † once; join with slip st to first dc: 78 dc and 18 ch-2 sps.

Rnd 7: Ch 3, 2 dc in same st, ★ † skip next 2 dc, 3 dc in sp **before** next dc, ch 2, (dc in next ch-2 sp, ch 2) twice, skip next 3 dc, 3 dc in sp **before** next dc, skip next 2 dc, 3 dc in next dc, ch 2 †, 3 dc in next dc; repeat from ★ 4 times **more**, then repeat from † to † once; join with slip st to first dc: 84 dc and 24 ch-2 sps.

Rnd 8: Ch 3, 2 dc in same st, ★ † skip next 2 dc, 3 dc in sp **before** next dc, ch 2, dc in next ch-2 sp, ch 2, 3 dc in next ch-2 sp, ch 2, dc in next ch-2 sp, ch 2, skip next 3 dc, 3 dc in sp **before** next dc, skip next 2 dc, 3 dc in next dc, ch 2 †, 3 dc in next dc; repeat from ★ 4 times **more**, then repeat from † to † once; join with slip st to first dc: 102 dc and 30 ch-2 sps.

Rnd 9: Ch 3, 2 dc in same st, ★ † skip next 2 dc, 3 dc in sp **before** next dc, ch 2, dc in next ch-2 sp, ch 2, 3 dc in each of next 2 ch-2 sps, ch 2, dc in next ch-2 sp, ch 2, skip next 3 dc, 3 dc in sp **before** next dc, skip next 2 dc, 3 dc in next dc, ch 2 †, 3 dc in next dc; repeat from ★ 4 times **more**, then repeat from † to † once; join with slip st to first dc: 120 dc and 30 ch-2 sps.

Rnd 10: Ch 3, 2 dc in same st, ★ † skip next 2 dc, 3 dc in sp **before** next dc, ch 2, dc in next ch-2 sp, ch 2, 3 dc in next ch-2 sp, skip next 3 dc, 3 dc in sp **before** next dc **and** in next ch-2 sp, ch 2, dc in next ch-2 sp, ch 2, skip next 3 dc, 3 dc in sp **before** next dc, skip next 2 dc, 3 dc in next dc, ch 2 †, 3 dc in next dc; repeat from ★ 4 times **more**, then repeat from † to † once; join with slip st to first dc: 138 dc and 30 ch-2 sps.

Rnd 11: Ch 3, 2 dc in same st, ★ † skip next 2 dc, 3 dc in sp **before** next dc, ch 2, dc in next ch-2 sp, ch 2, 3 dc in next ch-2 sp, (skip next 3 dc, 3 dc in sp **before** next dc) twice, 3 dc in next ch-2 sp, ch 2, dc in next ch-2 sp, ch 2, skip next 3 dc, 3 dc in sp **before** next dc, skip next 2 dc, 3 dc in next dc, ch 2 †, 3 dc in next dc; repeat from ★ 4 times **more**, then repeat from † to † once; join with slip st to first dc: 156 dc and 30 ch-2 sps.

Rnd 12: Ch 3, 2 dc in same st, ★ † skip next 2 dc, 3 dc in sp **before** next dc, ch 2, dc in next ch-2 sp, ch 2, 3 dc in next ch-2 sp, (skip next 3 dc, 3 dc in sp **before** next dc) 3 times, 3 dc in next ch-2 sp, ch 2, dc in next ch-2 sp, ch 2, skip next 3 dc, 3 dc in sp **before** next dc, skip next 2 dc, 3 dc in next dc, ch 2 †, 3 dc in next dc; repeat from ★ 4 times **more**, then repeat from † to † once; join with slip st to first dc: 174 dc and 30 ch-2 sps.

Rnd 13: Ch 3, 2 dc in same st, ★ † skip next 2 dc, 3 dc in sp **before** next dc, ch 2, (dc in next ch-2 sp, ch 2) twice, (skip next 3 dc, 3 dc in sp **before** next dc) 4 times, ch 2, (dc in next ch-2 sp, ch 2) twice, skip next 3 dc, 3 dc in sp **before** next dc, skip next 2 dc, 3 dc in next dc, ch 2 †, 3 dc in next dc; repeat from ★ 4 times **more**, then repeat from † to † once; join with slip st to first dc: 168 dc and 42 ch-2 sps.

Rnd 14: Ch 3, 2 dc in same st, ★ † skip next 2 dc, 3 dc in sp **before** next dc, ch 2, (dc in next ch-2 sp, ch 2) 3 times, (skip next 3 dc, 3 dc in sp **before** next dc) 3 times, ch 2, (dc in next ch-2 sp, ch 2) 3 times, skip next 3 dc, 3 dc in sp **before** next dc, skip next 2 dc, 3 dc in next dc, ch 2 †, 3 dc in next dc; repeat from ★ 4 times **more**, then repeat from † to † once; join with slip st to first dc: 162 dc and 54 ch-2 sps.

Rnd 15: Ch 3, 2 dc in same st, ★ † skip next 2 dc, 3 dc in sp **before** next dc, ch 2, (dc in next ch-2 sp, ch 2) 4 times, (skip next 3 dc, 3 dc in sp **before** next dc) twice, ch 2, (dc in next ch-2 sp, ch 2) 4 times, skip next 3 dc, 3 dc in sp **before** next dc, skip next 2 dc, 3 dc in next dc, ch 2 †, 3 dc in next dc; repeat from ★ 4 times **more**, then repeat from † to † once; join with slip st to first dc: 156 dc and 66 ch-2 sps.

Rnd 16: Slip st in next 2 dc and in sp **before** next dc, ch 3, 2 dc in same sp, ★ † 3 dc in next ch-2 sp, ch 2, (dc in next ch-2 sp, ch 2) 4 times, skip next 3 dc, 3 dc in sp **before** next dc, ch 2, (dc in next ch-2 sp, ch 2) 4 times, 3 dc in next ch-2 sp, skip next 3 dc, 3 dc in sp **before** next dc, ch 3, (dc, ch 3) 4 times in next ch-2 sp, skip next 3 dc †, 3 dc in sp **before** next dc; repeat from ★ 4 times **more**, then repeat from † to † once; join with slip st to first dc: 162 dc and 90 sps.

Rnd 17: Slip st in next 2 dc and in sp **before** next dc, ch 3, 2 dc in same sp, ★ † 3 dc in next ch-2 sp, ch 2, (dc in next ch-2 sp, ch 2) 3 times, 3 dc in each of next 2 ch-2 sps, ch 2, (dc in next ch-2 sp, ch 2) 3 times, 3 dc in next ch-2 sp, skip next 3 dc, 3 dc in sp **before** next dc, ch 3, (work 3-dc Cluster in next ch-3 sp, ch 3) 5 times, skip next 3 dc †, 3 dc in sp **before** next dc; repeat from ★ 4 times **more**, then repeat from † to † once; join with slip st to first dc: 174 sts and 84 sps.

Rnd 18: Slip st in next 2 dc and in sp **before** next dc, ch 3, 2 dc in same sp, ★ † 3 dc in next ch-2 sp, ch 2, (dc in next ch-2 sp, ch 2) twice, 3 dc in next ch-2 sp, skip next 3 dc, 3 dc in sp **before** next dc **and** in next ch-2 sp, ch 2, (dc in next ch-2 sp, ch 2) twice, 3 dc in next ch-2 sp, skip next 3 dc, 3 dc in sp **before** next dc, ch 3, sc in next ch-3 sp, (ch 5, sc in next ch-3 sp) 5 times, ch 3, skip next 3 dc †, 3 dc in sp **before** next dc; repeat from ★ 4 times **more**, then repeat from † to † once; join with slip st to first dc: 186 sts and 78 sps.

Rnd 19: Slip st in next 2 dc and in sp **before** next dc, ch 3, 2 dc in same sp, ★ † 3 dc in next ch-2 sp, ch 2, (dc in next ch-2 sp, ch 2) twice, (skip next 3 dc, 3 dc in sp **before** next dc) twice, ch 2, (dc in next ch-2 sp, ch 2) twice, 3 dc in next ch-2 sp, skip next 3 dc, 3 dc in sp **before** next dc, ch 3, work 3-dc Cluster in next ch-3 sp, (ch 5, work 3-dc Cluster in next sp) 6 times, ch 3, skip next 3 dc †, 3 dc in sp **before** next dc; repeat from ★ 4 times **more**, then repeat from † to † once; join with slip st to first dc: 174 sts and 84 sps.

Instructions continued on page 27.

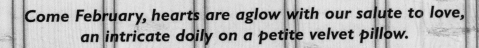

INTERMEDIATE

Finished Size: 6" (15 cm)

MATERIALS
Bedspread Weight Cotton Thread (size 10)
[225 yards (205.5 meters) per ball]: One ball
Steel crochet hook, size 6 (1.8 mm) **or** size
needed for gauge

GAUGE SWATCH: 1³/₄" (4.5 cm) diameter
Work same as Doily through Rnd 2.

STITCH GUIDE

TREBLE CROCHET (abbreviated tr)
YO twice, insert hook in st or sp indicated, YO and
pull up a loop (4 loops on hook), (YO and draw
through 2 loops on hook) 3 times **(Figs. 11a & b,
page 39)**.
PICOT
Ch 3, slip st in top of last tr made **(Fig. 14a,
page 39)**.

DOILY
Ch 6; join with slip st to form a ring.

Rnd 1 (Right side)**:** Ch 4 **(counts as first dc plus
ch 1)**, (dc in ring, ch 1) 11 times; join with slip st to first
dc: 12 dc and 12 ch-1 sps.

Rnd 2: (Slip st, ch 1, sc) in first ch-1 sp, (ch 7, sc in
next ch-1 sp) around, ch 3, tr in first sc to form last
ch-7 sp.

Rnd 3: Ch 1, sc in last ch-7 sp made, (ch 7, sc in next
ch-7 sp) around, ch 3, tr in first sc to form last ch-7 sp.

Rnd 4: Ch 3 **(counts as first dc)**, dc in last ch-7 sp
made, ch 4, (3 dc in next ch-7 sp, ch 4) around, dc in
same sp as first dc; join with slip st to first dc: 36 dc and
12 ch-4 sps.

Rnd 5: Ch 1, (sc, ch 1, hdc, dc, ch 1, dc) in first
ch-4 sp, ch 2, (tr, ch 1) 6 times in next ch-4 sp, (dc, ch 1,
hdc, ch 1, sc) in next ch-4 sp, [ch 1, skip next dc, sc in
next dc, (ch 1, sc) 3 times in next ch-4 sp] twice, ch 2,
skip next dc, hdc in next dc, ch 2, [(dc, ch 1) twice, tr]
in next ch-4 sp, ch 3 (point), [tr, (ch 1, dc) twice] in
next ch-4 sp, ch 2, skip next dc, hdc in next dc, ch 2,
[(sc, ch 1) 3 times in next ch-4 sp, skip next dc, sc in
next dc, ch 1] twice, (sc, ch 1, hdc, ch 1, dc) in next
ch-4 sp, (ch 1, tr) 6 times in next ch-4 sp, ch 2, (dc, ch 1,
dc, hdc, ch 1, sc) in next ch-4 sp, ch 1; join with slip st
to joining slip st: 51 sts and 49 sps.

Rnd 6: Sc in first ch-1 sp, hdc in next sc, 2 dc in
next ch-1 sp, dc in next 2 sts, 2 dc in next ch-1 sp, tr in
next dc, 3 tr in next ch-2 sp, (tr in next tr and in next
ch-1 sp) twice, (2 tr in next tr and in next ch-1 sp)
twice, (tr in next st and in next sp) 5 times, dc in next
sc, 2 dc in next ch-1 sp, (hdc in next sc and in next
ch-1 sp) 6 times, dc in next sc, (2 dc in next ch-2 sp,
dc in next st) twice, dc in next ch-1 sp, tr in next dc, tr
in next ch-1 sp and in next tr, (3 tr, ch 3, 3 tr) in next
ch-3 sp (point), tr in next tr, tr in next ch-1 sp and in
next dc, dc in next ch-1 sp and in next dc, (2 dc in next
ch-2 sp, dc in next st) twice, (hdc in next ch-1 sp and in
next sc) 6 times, 2 dc in next ch-1 sp, dc in next sc, (tr
in next sp and in next st) 5 times, (2 tr in next ch-1 sp
and in next tr) twice, (tr in next ch-1 sp and in next tr)
twice, 3 tr in next ch-2 sp, tr in next dc, 2 dc in next
ch-1 sp, dc in next 2 sts, 2 dc in next ch-1 sp, hdc in
next sc, sc in last ch-1 sp; do **not** join, place a 2" (5 cm)
piece of contrasting color thread before first st of next
rnd to mark beginning of rnd: 126 sts and one ch-3 sp.

Rnd 7: Sc in next 9 sts, 2 hdc in next tr, dc in next tr,
2 dc in next tr, dc in next 4 tr, 2 dc in next tr, (tr in
next 2 tr, 2 tr in next tr) twice, (tr in next 3 tr, 2 tr in
next tr) twice, tr in next 12 sts, dc in next 6 hdc, hdc in
next 8 dc, sc in next 6 tr, 5 sc in next ch-3 sp (point), sc
in next 6 tr, hdc in next 8 dc, dc in next 6 hdc, tr in
next 12 sts, (2 tr in next tr, tr in next 3 tr) twice, (2 tr
in next tr, tr in next 2 tr) twice, 2 dc in next tr, dc in
next 4 tr, 2 dc in next tr, dc in next tr, 2 hdc in next tr,
sc in next 9 sts: 145 sts.

Instructions continued on page 27.

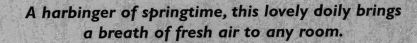

A harbinger of springtime, this lovely doily brings a breath of fresh air to any room.

Finished Size: 17" (43 cm) diameter

MATERIALS

Bedspread Weight Cotton Thread (size 10)
[284 yards (260 meters) per ball]: One ball
Steel crochet hook, size 7 (1.65 mm) **or** size
needed for gauge

GAUGE SWATCH: 2¹/₂" (6.25 cm) diameter
Work same as Doily through Rnd 3.

STITCH GUIDE

> **TREBLE CROCHET** *(abbreviated tr)*
> YO twice, insert hook in st or sp indicated, YO and
> pull up a loop (4 loops on hook), (YO and draw
> through 2 loops on hook) 3 times *(Figs. 11a & b,
> page 39)*.
> **PICOT**
> Ch 4, slip st in top of last st made *(Fig. 14a,
> page 39)*.

DOILY

Ch 8; join with slip st to form a ring.

Rnd 1 (Right side)**:** Ch 4 **(counts as first tr, now
and throughout)**, 23 tr in ring; join with slip st to first
tr: 24 tr.

Rnd 2: Ch 5 **(counts as first tr plus ch 1)**, (tr in
next tr, ch 1) around; join with slip st to first tr:
24 ch-1 sps.

Rnd 3: (Slip st, ch 4, 2 tr) in first ch-1 sp, ch 4, skip
next ch-1 sp, ★ 3 tr in next ch-1 sp, ch 4, skip next
ch-1 sp; repeat from ★ around; join with slip st to first
tr: 36 tr and 12 ch-4 sps.

Rnd 4: Ch 4, (tr, ch 3, tr) in next tr, tr in next tr,
★ ch 2, tr in next tr, (tr, ch 3, tr) in next tr, tr in next tr;
repeat from ★ around, hdc in first tr to form last
ch-2 sp: 24 sps.

Rnd 5: Ch 4, 2 tr in last ch-2 sp made, ch 4, (sc, work
Picot, sc) in next ch-3 sp, ch 4, ★ 3 tr in next ch-2 sp,
ch 4, (sc, work Picot, sc) in next ch-3 sp, ch 4; repeat
from ★ around; join with slip st to first tr: 36 tr.

Rnd 6: Ch 4, tr in next 2 tr, ch 9, skip next 2 ch-4 sps,
★ tr in next 3 tr, ch 9, skip next 2 ch-4 sps; repeat from
★ around; join with slip st to first tr: 36 tr and
12 ch-9 sps.

Rnd 7: Ch 4, (tr, ch 3, tr) in next tr, tr in next tr, ch 3,
skip next 3 chs, tr in next 3 chs, ch 3, ★ tr in next tr, (tr,
ch 3, tr) in next tr, tr in next tr, ch 3, skip next 3 chs, tr
in next 3 chs, ch 3; repeat from ★ around; join with
slip st to first tr: 84 tr and 36 ch-3 sps.

Rnd 8: Slip st in next tr and in next ch-3 sp, ch 4, (tr,
ch 3, 2 tr) in same sp, ch 4, skip next ch-3 sp, tr in next
3 tr, ch 4, skip next ch-3 sp, ★ (2 tr, ch 3, 2 tr) in next
ch-3 sp, ch 4, skip next ch-3 sp, tr in next 3 tr, ch 4, skip
next ch-3 sp; repeat from ★ around; join with slip st to
first tr.

Rnd 9: Slip st in next tr and in next ch-3 sp, ch 4, (tr,
ch 3, 2 tr) in same sp, ★ † ch 4, sc in next ch-4 sp, work
Picot, ch 4, skip next tr, tr in next tr, work Picot, ch 4, sc
in next ch-4 sp, work Picot, ch 4 †, (2 tr, ch 3, 2 tr) in
next ch-3 sp; repeat from ★ 10 times **more**, then
repeat from † to † once; join with slip st to first tr:
60 tr, 36 Picots, and 60 sps.

Rnd 10: Slip st in next tr and in next ch-3 sp, ch 4,
(tr, ch 3, 2 tr) in same sp, ch 4, skip next Picot, 6 tr in
next Picot (ch-4 sp), ch 4, skip next 2 ch-4 sps, ★ (2 tr,
ch 3, 2 tr) in next ch-3 sp, ch 4, skip next Picot, 6 tr in
next Picot, ch 4, skip next 2 ch-4 sps; repeat from ★
around; join with slip st to first tr: 120 tr and 36 sps.

Rnd 11: Slip st in next tr and in next ch-3 sp, ch 4,
(tr, ch 3, 2 tr) in same sp, ★ † ch 5, skip next ch-4 sp, sc
in next tr, (ch 4, sc in next tr) 5 times, ch 5, skip next
ch-4 sp †, (2 tr, ch 3, 2 tr) in next ch-3 sp; repeat from
★ 10 times **more**, then repeat from † to † once; join
with slip st to first tr: 120 sts and 96 sps.

Instructions continued on page 28.

Lovely lavender wisteria blooms inspired the design of this beautiful heirloom doily. Add a touch of tradition that helps protects your tabletop.

Finished Size: 15¹/₂" (39.5 cm) diameter

MATERIALS
Bedspread Weight Cotton Thread (size 10)
[252 yards (230 meters) per ball]: Two balls
Steel crochet hook, size 7 (1.65 mm) **or** size
   needed for gauge

GAUGE SWATCH: 2" (5 cm) diameter
Work same as Doily through Rnd 2.

STITCH GUIDE

TREBLE CROCHET *(abbreviated tr)*
YO twice, insert hook in st or sp indicated, YO and pull up a loop (4 loops on hook), (YO and draw through 2 loops on hook) 3 times *(Figs. 11a & b, page 39)*.

BEGINNING SPLIT CLUSTER (uses next 3 dc)
Ch 3, † YO twice, insert hook in **next** dc, YO and pull up a loop, (YO and draw through 2 loops on hook) twice †, skip next ch-3 sp, repeat from † to † twice, YO and draw through all 4 loops on hook.

SPLIT CLUSTER (uses next 4 dc)
† ★ YO twice, insert hook in **next** dc, YO and pull up a loop, (YO and draw through 2 loops on hook) twice; repeat from ★ once **more** †, skip next ch-3 sp, repeat from † to † once, YO and draw through all 5 loops on hook.

BEGINNING 3-TR CLUSTER
Ch 3, ★ YO twice, insert hook in ch-3 sp indicated, YO and pull up a loop, (YO and draw through 2 loops on hook) twice; repeat from ★ once **more**, YO and draw through all 3 loops on hook.

3-TR CLUSTER (uses one sp)
★ YO twice, insert hook in ch-3 sp indicated, YO and pull up a loop, (YO and draw through 2 loops on hook) twice; repeat from ★ 2 times **more**, YO and draw through all 4 loops on hook.

2-TR CLUSTER (uses next 2 tr)
★ YO twice, insert hook in **next** tr, YO and pull up a loop, (YO and draw through 2 loops on hook) twice; repeat from ★ once **more**, YO and draw through all 3 loops on hook.

POPCORN (uses one ch-2 sp)
5 Tr in ch-2 sp indicated, drop loop from hook, insert hook in first tr of 5-tr group, hook dropped loop and draw through st.
PICOT
Ch 4, slip st in top of last tr made *(Fig. 14a, page 39)*.

DOILY
Ch 5; join with slip st to form a ring.

Rnd 1 (Right side)**:** Ch 4 **(counts as first tr, now and throughout)**, 19 tr in ring; join with slip st to first tr: 20 tr.

Rnd 2: Ch 9, tr in next tr, (ch 5, tr in next tr) around, ch 2, dc in fourth ch of beginning ch-9 to form last ch-5 sp.

Rnd 3: Ch 1, sc in last ch-5 sp made, (ch 5, sc in next ch-5 sp) around, ch 2, dc in first sc to form last ch-5 sp.

Rnd 4: Ch 3 **(counts as first dc, now and throughout)**, dc in last ch-5 sp made, ch 3, (2 dc in next ch-5 sp, ch 3) around; join with slip st to first dc: 40 dc.

Rnd 5: Ch 3, 2 dc in next dc, ch 3, ★ dc in next dc, 2 dc in next dc, ch 3; repeat from ★ around; join with slip st to first dc: 60 dc.

Rnd 6: Ch 3, 2 dc in next dc, dc in next dc, ch 3, ★ dc in next dc, 2 dc in next dc, dc in next dc, ch 3; repeat from ★ around; join with slip st to first dc: 80 dc.

Rnd 7: Slip st in next 2 dc, work Beginning Split Cluster, (ch 7, work Split Cluster) around, ch 3, tr in top of Beginning Split Cluster to form last ch-7 sp: 20 ch-7 sps.

Rnd 8: Ch 6 **(counts as first dc plus ch 3)**, dc in last tr made, ch 5, skip next Split Cluster and next 3 chs, ★ (dc, ch 3, dc) in next ch, ch 5, skip next Split Cluster and next 3 chs; repeat from ★ around; join with slip st to first dc: 40 sps.

Instructions continued on page 28.

Our sunburst doily celebrates the fiesta of Cinco de Mayo with its dramatic size and festive intricate design.

Finished Size: 18" (35.5 cm) diameter

MATERIALS

Bedspread Weight Cotton Thread (size 10)
[350 yards (320 meters) per ball]: One ball
Steel crochet hook, size 6 (1.8 mm) **or** size
needed for gauge

GAUGE SWATCH: 1³/₄" (4.5 cm) diameter
Work same as Doily through Rnd 3.

STITCH GUIDE

TREBLE CROCHET (abbreviated tr)
YO twice, insert hook in st or sp indicated, YO and
pull up a loop (4 loops on hook), (YO and draw
through 2 loops on hook) 3 times **(Figs. 11a & b,
page 39)**.
DECREASE (uses 2 ch-3 sps)
★ YO, insert hook in **next** ch-3 sp, YO and pull up a
loop, YO and draw through 2 loops on hook; repeat
from ★ once **more**, YO and draw through all
3 loops on hook **(counts as one dc)**.

DOILY

Ch 10; join with slip st to form a ring.

Rnd 1 (Right side): Ch 4 **(counts as first dc plus
ch 1, now and throughout)**, (dc in ring, ch 1) 15
times; join with slip st to first dc: 16 ch-1 sps.

Rnd 2: (Slip st, ch 1, sc) in first ch-1 sp, (ch 4, sc in
next ch-1 sp) around, ch 2, hdc in first sc to form last
ch-2 sp.

Rnd 3: Ch 1, sc in last ch-4 sp made, (ch 4, sc in next
ch-4 sp) around, ch 1, dc in first sc to form last ch-4 sp.

Rnd 4: Ch 3 **(counts as first dc, now and
throughout)**, 2 dc in last ch-4 sp made, ch 3, sc in next
ch-4 sp, ch 3, ★ 3 dc in next ch-4 sp, ch 3, sc in next
ch-4 sp, ch 3; repeat from ★ around; join with slip st to
first dc: 32 sts and 16 ch-3 sps.

Rnd 5: Ch 1, sc in same st, ch 5, skip next dc, sc in
next dc and in next ch-3 sp, ch 3, ★ sc in next ch-3 sp
and in next dc, ch 5, skip next dc, sc in next dc and in
next ch-3 sp, ch 3; repeat from ★ around to last
ch-3 sp, sc in last ch-3 sp; join with slip st to first sc:
16 sps.

Rnd 6: (Slip st, ch 3, 8 dc) in first ch-5 sp, ch 3, sc in
next ch-3 sp, ch 3, ★ 9 dc in next ch-5 sp, ch 3, sc in
next ch-3 sp, ch 3; repeat from ★ around; join with
slip st to first dc: 80 sts and 16 ch-3 sps.

Rnd 7: Ch 4, dc in next dc, (ch 1, dc in next dc) 7
times, skip next 2 ch-3 sps, ★ dc in next dc, (ch 1, dc in
next dc) 8 times, skip next 2 ch-3 sps; repeat from ★
around; join with slip st to first dc: 72 dc and
64 ch-1 sps.

Rnd 8: (Slip st, ch 1, sc) in first ch-1 sp, (ch 4, sc in
next ch-1 sp) 7 times, ch 1, skip next dc, dc in sp
before next dc **(Fig. 13, page 39)**, ch 1, ★ sc in next
ch-1 sp, (ch 4, sc in next ch-1 sp) 7 times, ch 1, skip
next dc, dc in sp **before** next dc, ch 1; repeat from ★
around; join with slip st to first sc: 72 sts and 72 sps.

Rnd 9: (Slip st, ch 1, sc) in first ch-4 sp, ★ † (ch 4, sc
in next ch-4 sp) 6 times, ch 1, skip next sc, 3 dc in next
dc, ch 1, skip next ch-1 sp †, sc in next ch-4 sp; repeat
from ★ 6 times **more**, then repeat from † to † once;
join with slip st to first sc: 80 sts and 64 sps.

Rnd 10: (Slip st, ch 1, sc) in first ch-4 sp, ★ † (ch 4,
sc in next ch-4 sp) 5 times, ch 1, 3 dc in center dc of next
3-dc group, ch 1, skip next ch-1 sp †, sc in next ch-4 sp;
repeat from ★ 6 times **more**, then repeat from † to †
once; join with slip st to first sc: 72 sts and 56 sps.

Rnd 11: (Slip st, ch 1, sc) in first ch-4 sp, ★ † (ch 4, sc
in next ch-4 sp) 4 times, ch 1, (2 dc, ch 1) twice in
center dc of next 3-dc group, skip next ch-1 sp †, sc in
next ch-4 sp; repeat from ★ 6 times **more**, then repeat
from † to † once; join with slip st to first sc.

Instructions continued on page 30.

June

It's June and the wedding bells are pealing. This dazzling doily will be a treasured keepsake of that joyous commitment.

■■■□ INTERMEDIATE

Finished Size: 13" (33 cm) diameter

MATERIALS
Bedspread Weight Cotton Thread (size 10)
[400 yards (366 meters) per ball]: One ball
Steel crochet hook, size 7 (1.65 mm) **or** size needed for gauge

GAUGE SWATCH: 2" (5 cm) diameter
Work same as Doily through Rnd 4.

STITCH GUIDE

TREBLE CROCHET *(abbreviated tr)*
YO twice, insert hook in sc indicated, YO and pull up a loop (4 loops on hook), (YO and draw through 2 loops on hook) 3 times *(Figs. 11a & b, page 39)*.

DOUBLE TREBLE CROCHET
(abbreviated dtr)
YO 3 times, insert hook in sc indicated, YO and pull up a loop (5 loops on hook), (YO and draw through 2 loops on hook) 4 times *(Figs. 12a & b, page 39)*.

DECREASE
Pull up a loop in same sp as last sc made **and** in next sp, YO and draw through all 3 loops on hook.

PICOT
Ch 4, slip st in top of last decrease made *(Fig. 14b, page 39)*.

DOILY
Ch 8; join with slip st to form a ring.

Rnd 1 (Right side)**:** Ch 1, 24 hdc in ring; join with slip st to first hdc.

Rnd 2: Ch 4, (dc in next hdc, ch 1) around; join with slip st to third ch of beginning ch-4: 24 sts and 24 ch-1 sps.

Rnd 3: Ch 1, sc in same st, (ch 3, sc in next dc) around, ch 1, hdc in first sc to form last ch-3 sp.

Rnds 4 and 5: Ch 1, sc in last ch-3 sp made, (ch 3, sc in next ch-3 sp) around, ch 1, hdc in first sc to form last ch-3 sp.

Rnd 6: Ch 1, sc in last ch-3 sp made, ch 2, skip next sc and next ch, (slip st, ch 3, slip st, ch 5, slip st, ch 3, slip st) in next ch, ch 2, ★ sc in next ch-3 sp, ch 2, skip next sc and next ch, (slip st, ch 3, slip st, ch 5, slip st, ch 3, slip st) in next ch, ch 2; repeat from ★ around; join with slip st to first sc: 12 sc and 60 sps.

Rnd 7: Ch 1, sc in same st, ch 5, skip next 2 sps, sc in next ch-5 sp, ★ ch 5, skip next 2 sps, sc in next sc, ch 5, skip next 2 sps, sc in next ch-5 sp; repeat from ★ around to last 2 sps, ch 2, skip last 2 sps, dc in first sc to form last ch-5 sp: 24 sc and 24 ch-5 sps.

Rnd 8: Ch 1, 3 sc in last ch-5 sp made, slip st in next sc, 4 sc in next ch-5 sp, decrease, work Picot, ★ 4 sc in same sp as second half of decrease, slip st in next sc, 4 sc in next ch-5 sp, decrease, work Picot; repeat from ★ around, sc in same sp; join with slip st to first sc: 120 sts and 12 Picots.

Rnd 9: Ch 1, sc in same st, ch 5, skip next 5 sts, sc in next sc, ch 5, sc in next Picot, ★ ch 5, skip next sc, sc in next sc, ch 5, skip next 5 sts, sc in next sc, ch 5, sc in next Picot; repeat from ★ around, ch 2, dc in first sc to form last ch-5 sp: 36 sc and 36 ch-5 sps.

Rnd 10: Ch 1, 3 sc in last ch-5 sp made, sc in next ch-5 sp, 4 sc in next ch-5 sp, decrease, work Picot, ★ 4 sc in same sp as second half of decrease, sc in next ch-5 sp, 4 sc in next ch-5 sp, decrease, work Picot; repeat from ★ around, sc in same sp as second half of decrease; join with slip st to first sc: 120 sts and 12 Picots.

Rnd 11: Ch 1, sc in same st, ch 7, skip next 5 sc, sc in next sc, ★ ch 7, skip next Picot and next sc, sc in next sc, ch 7, skip next 5 sc, sc in next sc; repeat from ★ around to last Picot, ch 3, skip last Picot and last sc, tr in first sc to form last ch-7 sp: 24 ch-7 sps.

Rnd 12: Ch 1, sc in last ch-7 sp made, (ch 7, sc in next ch-7 sp) around, ch 3, tr in first sc to form last ch-7 sp.

Instructions continued on page 31.

Salute American independence with this rousing doily in concentric circles of red, white, and blue. It's a fitting tribute to summertime fun and a celebration of our land of liberty.

INTERMEDIATE

Finished Size: 12¹/₂" (31 cm) diameter

MATERIALS

Bedspread Weight Cotton Thread (size 10)
[400 yards (366 meters) per ball]:
   White - One ball
[350 yards (320 meters) per ball]:
   Red & Blue - One ball **each** color
Steel crochet hook, size 5 (1.9 mm) **or** size
   needed for gauge

GAUGE SWATCH: 2¹/₄" (5.75 cm) diameter
Work same as Doily through Rnd 3.

STITCH GUIDE

TREBLE CROCHET (abbreviated tr)
YO twice, insert hook in ch-3 sp indicated, YO and
pull up a loop (4 loops on hook), (YO and draw
through 2 loops on hook) 3 times **(Figs. 11a & b,
page 39)**.

**DOUBLE TREBLE CROCHET
   (abbreviated dtr)**
YO 3 times, insert hook in ch-5 sp indicated, YO
and pull up a loop (5 loops on hook), (YO and draw
through 2 loops on hook) 4 times **(Figs. 12a & b,
page 39)**.

PICOT
Ch 3, slip st in top of last dc made **(Fig. 14a,
page 39)**.

DOILY

With Red, ch 6; join with slip st to form a ring.

Rnd 1 (Right side): Ch 1, 2 sc in ring, (ch 5, 2 sc in
ring) 5 times, ch 2, dc in first sc to form last ch-5 sp:
12 sc and 6 ch-5 sps.

Note: Loop a short piece of thread around any stitch
to mark Rnd 1 as **right** side.

Rnd 2: Ch 1, sc in last ch-5 sp made, ch 6, (sc in next
ch-5 sp, ch 6) around; join with slip st to first sc.

Rnd 3: Ch 1, sc in same st, (3 sc, ch 3, 3 sc) in next
ch-6 sp, ★ sc in next sc, (3 sc, ch 3, 3 sc) in next
ch-6 sp; repeat from ★ around; join with slip st to first
sc: 42 sc and 6 ch-3 sps.

Rnd 4: Ch 1, sc in same st, ch 2, (2 tr, ch 2) 4 times in
next ch-3 sp, skip next 3 sc, ★ sc in next sc, ch 2, (2 tr,
ch 2) 4 times in next ch-3 sp, skip next 3 sc; repeat
from ★ around; join with slip st to first sc: 54 sts and
30 ch-2 sps.

Rnd 5: Slip st in next 2 chs and in next tr, ch 1, sc in
same st and in next tr, [(sc, ch 3, sc) in next ch-2 sp, sc
in next 2 tr] 3 times, skip next 2 ch-2 sps, ★ sc in next
2 tr, [(sc, ch 3, sc) in next ch-2 sp, sc in next 2 tr] 3
times, skip next 2 ch-2 sps; repeat from ★ around; join
with slip st to first sc: 18 ch-3 sps.

Rnd 6: Slip st in next 2 sc and in next ch-3 sp, ch 1,
3 sc in same sp, (ch 4, 3 sc in next ch-3 sp) twice, ch 1,
★ 3 sc in next ch-3 sp, (ch 4, 3 sc in next ch-3 sp)
twice, ch 1; repeat from ★ around; join with slip st to
first sc: 54 sc and 18 sps.

Rnd 7: Ch 1, sc in same st and in next 2 sc, [(sc, 2 dc,
work Picot, dc, sc) in next ch-3 sp, sc in next 3 sc]
twice, skip next ch, ★ sc in next 3 sc, [(sc, 2 dc, work
Picot, dc, sc) in next ch-3 sp, sc in next 3 sc] twice, skip
next ch; repeat from ★ around; join with slip st to first
sc, finish off: 12 Picots.

Rnd 8: With **right** side facing, join White with sc in
second Picot after joining **(see Joining With Sc,
page 39)**; ch 12, sc in next Picot, ch 10, ★ sc in next
Picot, ch 12, sc in next Picot, ch 10; repeat from ★
around; join with slip st to first sc: 12 loops.

Rnd 9: Ch 1, sc in same st, (6 sc, ch 5, 6 sc) in next
loop, sc in next sc, (5 sc, ch 3, 5 sc) in next loop, ★ sc in
next sc, (6 sc, ch 5, 6 sc) in next loop, sc in next sc,
(5 sc, ch 3, 5 sc) in next loop; repeat from ★ around;
join with slip st to first sc: 144 sc and 12 sps.

Instructions continued on page 32.

August

Cool shades of blue accented in white mimic the ebb and flow of water in this doily. What an appealing keepsake it will make for future generations!

Finished Size: 11½" (29 cm) diameter

MATERIALS
Bedspread Weight Cotton Thread (size 10)
[400 yards (366 meters) per ball]:
   White - One ball
[350 yards (320 meters) per ball]:
   Blue & Lt Blue - One ball **each** color
Steel crochet hook, size 7 (1.65 mm) **or** size
   needed for gauge
Sewing needle and thread

GAUGE SWATCH: 2½" (6.25 cm) diameter
Work same as Doily through Rnd 3.

STITCH GUIDE

TREBLE CROCHET (abbreviated tr)
YO twice, insert hook in st indicated, YO and pull up a loop (4 loops on hook), (YO and draw through 2 loops on hook) 3 times **(Figs. 11a & b, page 39)**.
SHELL
(2 Dc, 5 tr, 2 dc) in hdc indicated.
BEGINNING POPCORN (uses one st)
Ch 3 **(counts as first dc)**, 4 dc in st indicated, drop loop from hook, insert hook in first dc of 5-dc group, hook dropped loop and draw through st.
POPCORN (uses one st)
5 Dc in st indicated, drop loop from hook, insert hook in first dc of 5-dc group, hook dropped loop and draw through st.

DOILY

With Blue, ch 8; join with slip st to form a ring.

Rnd 1 (Right side)**:** Ch 3 **(counts as first dc, now and throughout)**, 23 dc in ring; join with slip st to first dc: 24 dc.

Note: Loop a short piece of thread around any stitch to mark Rnd 1 as **right** side.

Rnd 2: Ch 3, dc in same st, 2 dc in next dc and in each dc around; join with slip st to first dc: 48 dc.

Rnd 3: Ch 1, hdc in same st and in each dc around; join with slip st to first hdc.

Rnd 4: Ch 7, skip next 3 hdc, ★ slip st in next hdc, ch 7, skip next 3 hdc; repeat from ★ around; join with slip st to joining slip st: 12 ch-7 sps.

Rnd 5: Ch 1, 11 hdc in each ch-7 sp around; join with slip st to first ch: 132 hdc.

Rnd 6: Working **behind** previous 2 rnds and in skipped hdc on Rnd 3, slip st in first 2 hdc of first 3-hdc group, ch 11, (slip st in center hdc of next 3-hdc group, ch 11) around; join with slip st to second slip st: 12 loops.

Rnd 7: Ch 1, 19 hdc in each loop around; join with slip st to first hdc, finish off.

Rnd 8: With **right** side facing and working **behind** previous 4 rnds and in unworked hdc on Rnd 3, join Lt Blue with slip st in any hdc; ch 4 **(counts as first tr, now and throughout)**, 3 tr in same st, 4 tr in each hdc around; join with slip st to first tr: 96 tr.

Rnd 9: Ch 4, tr in next tr and in each tr around; join with slip st to first tr.

Rnd 10: Ch 1, hdc in same st and in each tr around; join with slip st to first hdc.

Rnd 11: Ch 3, dc in same st, ch 2, skip next hdc, ★ 2 dc in next hdc, ch 2, skip next hdc; repeat from ★ around; join with slip st to first dc: 96 dc and 48 ch-2 sps.

Rnd 12: Ch 1, hdc in same st and in next dc, 2 hdc in next ch-2 sp, (hdc in next 2 dc, 2 hdc in next ch-2 sp) around; join with slip st to first hdc: 192 hdc.

Instructions continued on page 33.

September

A deep red starburst marks the transition from summer to autumn and harvest time in this doily. It's a time for gathering the fruits of fall.

INTERMEDIATE

Finished Size: 15" (38 cm) from point to point

MATERIALS
Bedspread Weight Cotton Thread (size 10)
[350 yards (320 meters) per ball]: One ball
Steel crochet hook, size 7 (1.65 mm) **or** size needed for gauge

GAUGE SWATCH: 1³/₄" (4.5 cm) diameter
Work same as Doily through Rnd 4.

STITCH GUIDE

> **TREBLE CROCHET (abbreviated tr)**
> YO twice, insert hook in st indicated, YO and pull up a loop (4 loops on hook), (YO and draw through 2 loops on hook) 3 times **(Figs. 11a & b, page 39)**.

DOILY

Ch 8; join with slip st to form a ring.

Rnd 1 (Right side)**:** Ch 1, 16 sc in ring; join with slip st to first sc.

Rnd 2: Ch 4, (dc in next sc, ch 1) around; join with slip st to third ch of beginning ch-4: 16 sts and 16 ch-1 sps.

Rnd 3: Ch 1, sc in same st and in each ch-1 sp and each dc around; join with slip st to first sc: 32 sc.

Rnd 4: Ch 1, 2 sc in same st and in each sc around; join with slip st to first sc: 64 sc.

Rnd 5: Ch 1, sc in same st, ★ ch 3, skip next sc, sc in next sc; repeat from ★ around to last sc, ch 1, skip last sc, hdc in first sc to form last ch-3 sp: 32 ch-3 sps.

Rnds 6-9: Ch 1, sc in last ch-3 sp made, (ch 3, sc in next ch-3 sp) around, ch 1, hdc in first sc to form last ch-3 sp.

Rnd 10: Ch 1, sc in last ch-3 sp made, ch 3, (sc in next ch-3 sp, ch 3) around; join with slip st to first sc.

Rnd 11: Ch 1, sc in same st, 3 sc in next ch-3 sp, (sc in next sc, 3 sc in next ch-3 sp) around; join with slip st to first sc: 128 sc.

Rnd 12: Ch 1, sc in same st and in each sc around; join with slip st to first sc.

Rnd 13: Ch 1, sc in same st, ★ ch 5, skip next 3 sc, sc in next sc; repeat from ★ around to last 3 sc, ch 2, skip last 3 sc, dc in first sc to form last ch-5 sp: 32 ch-5 sps.

Rnd 14: Ch 1, sc in top of last dc made, ch 1, working in center ch of each ch-5 around, 11 tr in next center ch, ch 1, sc in next center ch, ★ (ch 5, sc in next center ch) twice, ch 1, 11 tr in next center ch, ch 1, sc in next center ch; repeat from ★ around to last ch-5, ch 5, sc in next center ch, ch 2, dc in first sc to form last ch-5 sp: 112 sts and 32 sps.

Rnd 15: Ch 1, sc in last ch-5 sp made, ★ † ch 1, skip next sc, (dc in next tr, ch 1) 11 times, sc in next ch-5 sp †, ch 5, sc in next ch-5 sp; repeat from ★ 6 times **more**, then repeat from † to † once, ch 2, dc in first sc to form last ch-5 sp: 104 sps.

Rnd 16: Ch 3 **(counts as first dc, now and throughout)**, 2 dc in last ch-5 sp made, ★ † ch 1, skip next ch-1 sp, sc in next ch-1 sp, (ch 4, sc in next ch-1 sp) 9 times, ch 1, skip next ch-1 sp †, (3 dc, ch 3, 3 dc) in next ch-5 sp; repeat from ★ 6 times **more**, then repeat from † to † once, 3 dc in same sp as first dc, ch 1, hdc in first dc to form last ch-3 sp: 96 sps.

Rnd 17: Ch 3, 2 dc in last ch-3 sp made, ★ † ch 1, skip next ch-1 sp, sc in next ch-4 sp, (ch 4, sc in next ch-4 sp) 8 times, ch 1, skip next ch-1 sp †, (3 dc, ch 3, 3 dc) in next ch-3 sp; repeat from ★ 6 times **more**, then repeat from † to † once, 3 dc in same sp as first dc, ch 1, hdc in first dc to form last ch-3 sp: 88 sps.

Rnd 18: Ch 3, 2 dc in last ch-3 sp made, ★ † ch 1, skip next ch-1 sp, sc in next ch-4 sp, (ch 4, sc in next ch-4 sp) 7 times, ch 1, skip next ch-1 sp †, (3 dc, ch 3, 3 dc) in next ch-3 sp; repeat from ★ 6 times **more**, then repeat from † to † once, 3 dc in same sp as first dc, ch 1, hdc in first dc to form last ch-3 sp: 80 sps.

Instructions continued on page 34.

October

Halloween weaves its mysterious web in this selection made with black thread. It will be a focal point of your favorite fall holiday for many years to come.

■■■□ INTERMEDIATE

Finished Size: 15" (38 cm) from point to point

MATERIALS

Bedspread Weight Cotton Thread (size 10)
[350 yards (320 meters) per ball]: One ball
Steel crochet hook, size 6 (1.8 mm) **or** size
    needed for gauge

GAUGE SWATCH: 2" (5 cm) diameter
Work same as Doily through Rnd 2.

STITCH GUIDE

TREBLE CROCHET *(abbreviated tr)*
YO twice, insert hook in st or sp indicated, YO and
pull up a loop (4 loops on hook), (YO and draw
through 2 loops on hook) 3 times *(Figs. 11a & b, page 39)*.

DOUBLE TREBLE CROCHET
    (abbreviated dtr)
YO 3 times, insert hook in st indicated, YO and pull
up a loop (5 loops on hook), (YO and draw through
2 loops on hook) 4 times *(Figs. 12a & b, page 39)*.

BEGINNING POPCORN (uses one st or sp)
Ch 4 **(counts as first tr)**, 4 tr in st or sp indicated,
drop loop from hook, insert hook in first tr of
5-tr group, hook dropped loop and draw through st.

POPCORN (uses one st or sp)
5 Tr in st or sp indicated, drop loop from hook,
insert hook in first dc of 5-tr group, hook dropped
loop and draw through st.

DOILY

Ch 8; join with slip st to form a ring.

Rnd 1 (Right side)**:** Ch 1, 16 sc in ring; join with slip st
to first sc.

Rnd 2: Ch 5 **(counts as first dtr, now and
throughout)**, dtr in next sc, ch 7, (dtr in next 2 sc,
ch 7) around; join with slip st to first dtr: 16 dtr and
8 ch-7 sps.

Rnd 3: Ch 1, sc in same st and in next dtr, 6 sc in
next ch-7 sp, (sc in next 2 dtr, 6 sc in next ch-7 sp)
around; join with slip st to first sc: 64 sc.

Rnd 4: Ch 5, dtr in next sc, ★ ch 5, skip next 2 sc, dtr
in next 2 sc; repeat from ★ around to last 2 sc, ch 2,
skip last 2 sc, dc in first dtr to form last ch-5 sp: 32 dtr
and 16 ch-5 sps.

Rnd 5: Ch 1, 2 sc in last ch-5 sp made, sc in next
2 dtr, (4 sc in next ch-5 sp, sc in next 2 dtr) around;
2 sc in same sp as first sc; join with slip st to Back Loop
Only of first sc *(Fig. 1)*: 96 sc.

Fig. 1

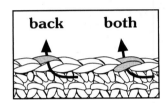

back   both

Rnd 6: Ch 1, sc in Back Loop Only of same st and
each sc around; join with slip st to **both** loops of first sc.

Rnd 7: Ch 1, working in both loops, sc in same st,
★ ch 9, skip next 5 sc, sc in next sc; repeat from ★
around to last 5 sc, ch 4, skip last 5 sc, dtr in first sc
to form last ch-9 sp: 16 ch-9 sps.

Rnd 8: Work Beginning Popcorn in top of last dtr
made, ch 5, sc in last ch-9 sp made, ch 5, ★ sc in next
ch-9 sp, ch 5, work Popcorn in center ch of same ch-9,
ch 5, sc in same ch-9 sp, ch 5; repeat from ★ around, sc
in same sp as Beginning Popcorn, ch 3, hdc in top of
Beginning Popcorn to form last ch-5 sp: 48 ch-5 sps.

Rnd 9: Ch 1, sc in last ch-5 sp made, ch 5, sc in next
ch-5 sp, ch 5, work Popcorn in center ch of next ch-5,
★ ch 5, (sc in next ch-5 sp, ch 5) twice, work Popcorn
in center ch of next ch-5; repeat from ★ around, ch 2,
dc in first sc to form last ch-5 sp.

Instructions continued on page 35.

Displayed in a beautiful custom frame, this "our-daily" bread doily commemorates the traditional feast of Thanksgiving with softspoken elegance.

Finished Size: 9¹/₂" x 19¹/₂" (24 cm x 49.5 cm)

MATERIALS

Bedspread Weight Cotton Thread (size 10) **[284 yards (260 meters) per ball]**: One ball Steel crochet hook, size 6 (1.8 mm) **or** size needed for gauge

GAUGE SWATCH: 2¹/₄" (5.75 cm) square
Ch 20.
Row 1: Dc in fourth ch from hook **(3 skipped chs count as first dc)** and in each ch across: 18 dc.
Rows 2-8: Ch 3 **(counts as first dc)**, turn; dc in next dc and in each dc across.
Finish off.

STITCH GUIDE

BLOCK OVER SPACE
2 Dc in next ch-2 sp, dc in next dc.
BLOCK OVER BLOCK
Dc in next 3 dc.
BEGINNING SPACE OVER SPACE
Ch 5 **(counts as first dc plus ch 2)**, turn; dc in next dc.
SPACE OVER BLOCK
Ch 2, skip next 2 dc, dc in next dc.
SPACE OVER SPACE
Ch 2, dc in next dc.
BEGINNING BLOCK DECREASE
Turn; slip st in next 3 sts, ch 3 **(counts as first dc)**.

DOILY

Ch 56.

Row 1 (Right side)**:** Dc in eighth ch from hook, place marker around dc just made for Short End joining placement, ★ ch 2, skip next 2 chs, dc in next ch; repeat from ★ across: 17 dc and 17 sps.

Note: Loop a short piece of thread around any stitch to mark Row 1 as **right** side.

Row 2: Work Beginning Space Over Space, work Space Over Space across to last sp, ch 2, skip next 2 chs, dc in next ch: 17 Spaces.

Row 3: Work Beginning Space Over Space, work 3 Spaces, work Block Over Space, work 7 Spaces, work Block, work 4 Spaces.

Rows 4-44: Follow chart.

Instructions continued on page 36.

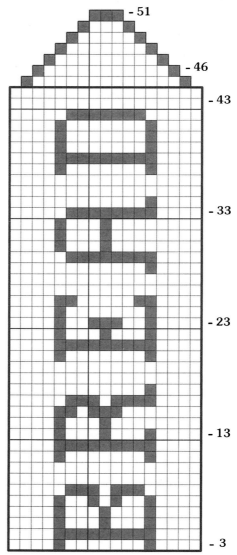

- 51
- 46
- 43
- 33
- 23
- 13
- 3

KEY

▨	- Block
☐	- Space

On **even-numbered** rows, follow chart from **left** to **right**.
On **odd-numbered** rows, follow chart from **right** to **left**.

December

INTERMEDIATE

December's doily of choice makes a thoughtful and cherished gift: a feminine sachet in cool shades of blue. It's the sure way to make spirits bright this holiday!

Finished Size: 6¹/₂" (16.5 cm) diameter

MATERIALS

Bedspread Weight Cotton Thread (size 10)
[284 yards (260 meters) per ball]:
    Blue & Lt Blue - One ball **each** color
Steel crochet hook, size 6 (1.8 mm) **or** size needed for gauge
6" x 12" (15 cm x 30.5 cm) piece of satin
Potpourri - small amount
Tapestry needle
Sewing needle and thread

GAUGE SWATCH: 1⁷/₈" (4.75 cm) diameter
Work same as Doily/Sachet Back through Rnd 4.

STITCH GUIDE

TREBLE CROCHET (abbreviated tr)
YO twice, insert hook in st or sp indicated, YO and pull up a loop (4 loops on hook), (YO and draw through 2 loops on hook) 3 times **(Figs. 11a & b, page 39)**.

CLUSTER (uses one dc)
★ YO, insert hook in dc indicated, YO and pull up a loop, YO and draw through 2 loops on hook; repeat from ★ 2 times **more**, YO and draw through all 4 loops on hook.

FRONT POST SINGLE CROCHET
    (abbreviated FPsc)
Insert hook from **front** to **back** around post of Split FPtr indicated **(Fig. 2)**, YO and pull up a loop even with last st made, YO and draw through both loops on hook.

Fig. 2

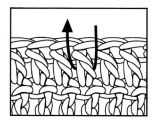

FRONT POST DOUBLE CROCHET
    (abbreviated FPdc)
YO, insert hook from **front** to **back** around post of Cluster indicated **(Fig. 2)**, YO and pull up a loop (3 loops on hook), (YO and draw through 2 loops on hook) twice.

FRONT POST TREBLE CROCHET
    (abbreviated FPtr)
YO twice, insert hook from **front** to **back** around post of FPsc indicated **(Fig. 2)**, YO and pull up a loop (4 loops on hook), (YO and draw through 2 loops on hook) 3 times.

SPLIT FRONT POST TREBLE CROCHET
(abbreviated Split FPtr)
First Leg: YO twice, working in **front** of previous rnd, insert hook from **front** to **back** around post of dc indicated **(Fig. 2)**, YO and pull up a loop, (YO and draw through 2 loops on hook) twice (2 loops remaining on hook).
Second Leg: YO twice, skip next Cluster, insert hook from **front** to **back** around post of next dc, YO and pull up a loop, (YO and draw through 2 loops on hook) twice, YO and draw through all 3 loops on hook.

TWISTED SPLIT TR
First Leg: YO twice, working in **front** of previous rnds, insert hook in ch-5 sp indicated, YO and pull up a loop, (YO and draw through 2 loops on hook) twice (2 loops remaining on hook).
Second Leg: YO twice, working in **front** of First Leg and previous rnds, insert hook in ch-5 sp indicated, YO and pull up a loop, (YO and draw through 2 loops on hook) twice, YO and draw through all 3 loops on hook.

PICOT
Ch 3, slip st in third ch from hook, ch 1.

DOILY SACHET
FRONT

Rnd 1 (Right side): With Blue, ch 4, 11 dc in fourth ch from hook **(3 skipped chs count as first dc)**; join with slip st to first dc: 12 dc.

Note: Loop a short piece of thread around any stitch to mark Rnd 1 as **right** side.

Instructions continued on page 26.

Rnd 2: Ch 5 **(counts as first dc plus ch 2)**, work Cluster in next dc, ch 2, ★ dc in next dc, ch 2, work Cluster in next dc, ch 2; repeat from ★ around; join with slip st to first dc: 12 sts and 12 ch-2 sps.

Rnd 3: Ch 3 **(counts as first dc, now and throughout)**, dc in same st, 2 dc in next ch-2 sp, work FPdc around next Cluster, 2 dc in next ch-2 sp, ★ 2 dc in next dc and in next ch-2 sp, work FPdc around next Cluster, 2 dc in next ch-2 sp; repeat from ★ around; join with slip st to first dc: 42 sts.

Rnd 4: Ch 1, sc in same st and in next 3 dc, work First Leg of Split FPtr around first dc on Rnd 2, ★ work Second Leg around next dc, skip next FPdc on Rnd 3 from last sc made, sc in next 6 dc, work First Leg of Split FPtr around same st as Second Leg of last Split FPtr made; repeat from ★ 4 times **more**, working **above** previous st, work Second Leg around same st as First Leg of first Split FPtr made, skip next FPdc on Rnd 3 from last sc made, sc in last 2 dc; join with slip st to first sc.

Rnd 5: Ch 4 **(counts as first tr)**, tr in same st, 3 tr in next sc, ★ † 2 dc in next sc, hdc in next sc, work FPsc around next Split FPtr, hdc in next sc, 2 dc in next sc †, 3 tr in each of next 2 sc; repeat from ★ 4 times **more**, then repeat from † to † once, tr in same st as first tr; join with slip st to first tr: 78 sts.

Rnd 6: Ch 1, sc in same st, (ch 5, skip next 2 sts, sc in next st) twice, ch 1, skip next 3 sts, sc in next dc, ★ (ch 5, skip next 2 sts, sc in next st) 3 times, ch 1, skip next 3 sts, sc in next dc; repeat from ★ around to last 2 sts, ch 1, skip last 2 sts, tr in first sc to form last ch-5 sp: 24 sps.

Rnd 7: Ch 1, sc in last ch-5 sp made, ★ † ch 5, (sc, ch 5) twice in next ch-5 sp, sc in next ch-5 sp and in next sc, working in **front** of next ch-1, work FPtr around skipped FPsc on Rnd 5 †, sc in next sc on Rnd 6 and in next ch-5 sp; repeat from ★ 4 times **more**, then repeat from † to † once, sc in last sc on Rnd 6; join with slip st to first sc: 42 sts and 18 ch-5 sps.

Rnd 8: Ch 1, sc in same st, ★ † 2 sc in next ch-5 sp, ch 5, 3 sc in next ch-5 sp, ch 5, 2 sc in next ch-5 sp, sc in next 2 sc, skip next FPtr †, sc in next 2 sc; repeat from ★ 4 times **more**, then repeat from † to † once, sc in last sc; join with slip st to first sc: 66 sts and 12 ch-5 sps.

Rnd 9: Ch 1, sc in same st, ★ † working in **front** of previous rnds, tr in first ch-5 sp on Rnd 6 (after sc), skip next sc on Rnd 8 from last sc made , sc in next sc, 4 sc in next ch-5 sp, sc in next 3 sc, 4 sc in next ch-5 sp, sc in next sc, working in **front** of previous rnds, skip next ch-5 sp on Rnd 6, tr in next ch-5 sp (before sc), skip next sc on Rnd 8 from last sc made, sc in next sc, skip next 2 sc †, sc in next sc; repeat from ★ 4 times **more**, then repeat from † to † once; join with slip st to first sc: 102 sts.

Rnd 10: Slip st in next tr, ch 1, sc in same st and in next 6 sc, ★ † work First Leg of Twisted Split tr in third ch-5 sp of 3 ch-5 sp group on Rnd 7 and Second Leg in first ch-5 sp of same group, skip next sc on Rnd 9 from last sc made, sc in next 7 sts, skip next 2 sc †, sc in next 7 sts; repeat from ★ 4 times **more**, then repeat from † to † once; join with slip st to first sc: 90 sts.

Rnd 11: Ch 3, dc in next sc, hdc in next sc, sc in next 9 sts, hdc in next sc, ★ dc in next 4 sts, hdc in next sc, sc in next 9 sts, hdc in next sc; repeat from ★ around to last 2 sc, dc in last 2 sc; join with slip st to first dc, finish off.

Rnd 12: With **right** side facing, join Lt Blue with sc in same st as joining **(see Joining With Sc, page 39)**; ★ ch 5, skip next 2 sts, sc in next st; repeat from ★ around to last 2 sts, ch 2, skip last 2 sts, dc in first sc to form last ch-5 sp: 30 ch-5 sps.

Rnds 13 and 14: Ch 1, sc in last ch-5 sp made, (ch 5, sc in next ch-5 sp) around, ch 2, dc in first sc to form last ch-5 sp.

Rnd 15: Ch 1, 3 sc in last ch-5 sp made, (ch 3, 3 sc in next ch-5 sp) around, ch 1, hdc in first sc to form last ch-3 sp.

Rnd 16: Ch 1, sc in last ch-5 sp made, 9 tr in next ch-3 sp, (sc in next ch-3 sp, 9 tr in next ch-3 sp) around; join with slip st to first sc: 150 sts.

Rnd 17: Sc in next tr, ★ † work Picot, skip next tr, sc in next tr, work Picot, skip next tr, (dc, work Picot) twice in next tr, skip next tr, sc in next tr, work Picot, skip next tr, sc in next tr †, slip st in next sc, sc in next tr; repeat from ★ 13 times **more**, then repeat from † to † once; join with slip st to joining slip st, finish off.

BACK
Rnds 1-11: Work same as Front.

See Washing and Blocking, page 39.

POTPOURRI POUCH
Using Back as a pattern, cut 2 pieces from satin ¼" (6 mm) larger than pattern. With **right** sides together, sew both pieces together using ¼" (6 mm) seam allowance and leaving a 1½" (4 cm) opening. Turn right side out. Fill Pouch with potpourri and sew opening closed.

With **wrong** sides of Back and Front together and working through inside loops of sts on Rnd 11 **(Fig. 3)**, sew Back and Front together inserting pouch before closing.

Fig. 3

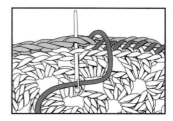

Design by Sarah J. Green.

JANUARY
Instructions continued from page 3.

Rnd 20: Slip st in next 2 dc and in sp **before** next dc, ch 3, 2 dc in same sp, ★ † 3 dc in next ch-2 sp, ch 2, (dc in next ch-2 sp, ch 2) twice, skip next 3 dc, 3 dc in sp **before** next dc, ch 2, (dc in next ch-2 sp, ch 2) twice, 3 dc in next ch-2 sp, skip next 3 dc, 3 dc in sp **before** next dc, ch 3, dc in next ch-3 sp, (ch 5, dc in next sp) 7 times, ch 3, skip next 3 dc †, 3 dc in sp **before** next dc; repeat from ★ 4 times **more**, then repeat from † to † once; join with slip st to first dc: 162 sts and 90 sps.

Rnd 21: Slip st in next 2 dc and in sp **before** next dc, ch 3, 2 dc in same sp, ★ † 3 dc in next ch-2 sp, ch 2, (dc in next ch-2 sp, ch 2) 4 times, 3 dc in next ch-2 sp, skip next 3 dc, 3 dc in sp **before** next dc, ch 5, (work 4-tr Cluster in next sp, ch 5) 9 times, skip next 3 dc †, 3 dc in sp **before** next dc; repeat from ★ 4 times **more**, then repeat from † to † once; join with slip st to first dc: 150 sts and 90 sps.

Rnd 22: Slip st in next 2 dc and in sp **before** next dc, ch 3, 2 dc in same sp, ★ † 3 dc in next ch-2 sp, ch 2, (dc in next ch-2 sp, ch 2) 3 times, 3 dc in next ch-2 sp, skip next 3 dc, 3 dc in sp **before** next dc, **turn**; slip st in first 3 dc and in sp **before** next dc, ch 3, 2 dc in same sp, 3 dc in next ch-2 sp, ch 2, (dc in next ch-2 sp, ch 2) twice, 3 dc in next ch-2 sp, skip next 3 dc, 3 dc in sp **before** next dc, **turn**; slip st in first 3 dc and in sp **before** next dc, ch 3, 2 dc in same sp, 3 dc in next ch-2 sp, ch 2, dc in next ch-2 sp, ch 2, 3 dc in next ch-2 sp, skip next 3 dc, 3 dc in sp **before** next dc, **turn**; slip st in first 3 dc and in sp **before** next dc, ch 3, 2 dc in same sp, 3 dc in each of next 2 ch-2 sps, skip next 3 dc, 3 dc in sp **before** next dc, **turn**; slip st in first 3 dc and in sp **before** next dc, ch 3, 2 dc in same sp, (skip next 3 dc, 3 dc in sp **before** next dc) twice, **turn**; slip st in first 3 dc and in sp **before** next dc, ch 3, 2 dc in same sp, skip next 3 dc, 3 dc in sp **before** next dc, **turn**; slip st in first 3 dc and in sp **before** next dc, ch 3, 2 dc in same sp, ch 3, do **not** turn; (skip next 2 dc at end of previous row, sc in last dc, ch 3) 6 times, sc in next ch-5 sp, (ch 7, sc in next sp) 9 times, ch 3, skip next 3 dc †, 3 dc in sp **before** next dc; repeat from ★ 4 times **more**, then repeat from † to † once; join with slip st to first dc.

Rnd 23: Ch 1, sc in same st, ch 3, ★ working in end of rows, (sc in top first dc on next row, ch 3) 6 times, skip next dc, sc in next dc, ch 3, (sc in next sc, ch 3) 5 times, skip next 2 ch-3 sps, sc in next ch-7 sp, (ch 9, sc in next ch-7 sp) 8 times, ch 3, skip next 3 dc; repeat from ★ around; join with slip st to first sc, finish off.

See Washing and Blocking, page 39.

Design by Darlene Polachic.

FEBRUARY
Instructions continued from page 4.

Rnd 8: Slip st in next sc, sc in next 4 sc, [ch 3, skip next 3 sts, (2 tr, work Picot, 2 tr) in next st, ch 3, skip next 3 sts, slip st in next st] 8 times, ch 4, skip next 3 sc, (2 tr, work Picot, 2 tr) in next sc, ch 4, skip next 3 sc, [slip st in next st, ch 3, skip next 3 sts, (2 tr, work Picot, 2 tr) in next st, ch 3, skip next 3 sts] 8 times, sc in next 4 sc; slip st in next sc, finish off.

See Washing and Blocking, page 39.

Design by Nancy L. Fuller.

MARCH
Instructions continued from page 6.

Rnd 12: Slip st in next tr and in next ch-3 sp, ch 4, (tr, ch 3, 2 tr) in same sp, ★ † ch 5, skip next ch-5 sp, sc in next ch-4 sp, (ch 4, sc in next ch-4 sp) 4 times, ch 5, skip next ch-5 sp †, (2 tr, ch 3, 2 tr) in next ch-3 sp; repeat from ★ 10 times **more**, then repeat from † to † once; join with slip st to first tr: 108 sts and 84 sps.

Rnd 13: Slip st in next tr and in next ch-3 sp, ch 4, (tr, ch 3, 2 tr) in same sp, ★ † ch 6, skip next ch-5 sp, sc in next ch-4 sp, (ch 4, sc in next ch-4 sp) 3 times, ch 6, skip next ch-5 sp †, (2 tr, ch 3, 2 tr) in next ch-3 sp; repeat from ★ 10 times **more**, then repeat from † to † once; join with slip st to first tr: 96 sts and 72 sps.

Rnd 14: Slip st in next tr and in next ch-3 sp, ch 4, [tr, (ch 3, 2 tr) twice] in same sp, ★ † ch 6, skip next ch-6 sp, sc in next ch-4 sp, (ch 4, sc in next ch-4 sp) twice, ch 6, skip next ch-6 sp †, 2 tr in next ch-3 sp, (ch 3, 2 tr in same sp) twice; repeat from ★ 10 times **more**, then repeat from † to † once; join with slip st to first tr: 108 sts and 72 sps.

Rnd 15: Slip st in next tr and in next ch-3 sp, ch 4, (tr, ch 3, 2 tr) in same sp, ★ † ch 6, slip st in third ch from hook (Small Picot made), ch 3, (2 tr, ch 3, 2 tr) in next ch-3 sp, ch 6, skip next ch-6 sp, sc in next ch-4 sp, ch 4, sc in next ch-4 sp, ch 6, skip next ch-6 sp †, (2 tr, ch 3, 2 tr) in next ch-3 sp; repeat from ★ 10 times **more**, then repeat from † to † once; join with slip st to first tr: 120 sts, 12 Picots, and 84 sps.

Rnd 16: Slip st in next tr and in next ch-3 sp, ch 4, (tr, ch 3, 2 tr) in same sp, ★ † ch 3, skip next ch-3 sp, 6 tr in next Small Picot, ch 3, skip next ch-3 sp, (2 tr, ch 3, 2 tr) in next ch-3 sp, ch 6, skip next ch-6 sp, sc in next ch-4 sp, ch 6, skip next ch-6 sp †, (2 tr, ch 3, 2 tr) in next ch-3 sp; repeat from ★ 10 times **more**, then repeat from † to † once; join with slip st to first tr: 180 sts and 72 sps.

Rnd 17: Slip st in next tr and in next ch-3 sp, ch 4, (tr, ch 3, 2 tr) in same sp, ★ † ch 3, skip next ch-3 sp, 2 tr in each of next 6 tr, ch 3, skip next ch-3 sp, (2 tr, ch 3, 2 tr) in next ch-3 sp, ch 6, skip next ch-6 sp, sc in next sc, ch 6, skip next ch-6 sp †, (2 tr, ch 3, 2 tr) in next ch-3 sp; repeat from ★ 10 times **more**, then repeat from † to † once; join with slip st to first tr: 252 sts and 72 sps.

Rnd 18: Slip st in next tr and in next ch-3 sp, ch 4, (tr, ch 3, 2 tr) in same sp, ★ † ch 4, skip next ch-3 sp, tr in next 3 tr, (ch 3, tr in next 3 tr) 3 times, ch 4, skip next ch-3 sp, (2 tr, ch 3, 2 tr) in next ch-3 sp, skip next 2 ch-6 sps †, (2 tr, ch 3, 2 tr) in next ch-3 sp; repeat from ★ 10 times **more**, then repeat from † to † once; join with slip st to first tr: 240 tr and 84 sps.

Rnd 19: Slip st in next tr and in next ch-3 sp, ch 4, (tr, ch 3, 2 tr) in same sp, ★ † ch 4, skip next ch-4 sp, [tr in next tr, (tr, ch 3, tr) in next tr, tr in next tr, ch 4] 4 times, skip next ch-4 sp †, (2 tr, ch 3, 2 tr) in next 2 ch-3 sps; repeat from ★ 10 times **more**, then repeat from † to † once, (2 tr, ch 3, 2 tr) in last ch-3 sp; join with slip st to first tr: 288 tr and 132 sps.

Rnd 20: Slip st in next tr and in next ch-3 sp, ch 1, sc in same sp, ★ † [ch 4, (2 tr, work Picot, tr) in next ch-4 sp, ch 4, sc next ch-3 sp] 5 times, skip next 2 tr, (2 tr, work Picot, tr) in sp **before** next tr *(Fig. 13, page 39)* †, sc in next ch-3 sp; repeat from ★ 10 times **more**, then repeat from † to † once; join with slip st to first sc, finish off.

See Washing and Blocking, page 39.

Design by Margaret Rost.

APRIL
Instructions continued from page 8.

Rnd 9: (Slip st, ch 3, 3 dc) in first ch-3 sp, ch 4, sc in next ch-5 sp, ch 4, ★ 4 dc in next ch-3 sp, ch 4, sc in next ch-5 sp, ch 4; repeat from ★ around; join with slip st to first dc: 100 sts and 40 ch-4 sps.

Rnd 10: (Slip st, ch 1, sc) in next dc, sc in next dc, ch 5, skip next ch-4 sp, tr in next sc, ch 5, skip next ch-4 sp and next dc, ★ sc in next 2 dc, ch 5, skip next ch-4 sp, tr in next sc, ch 5, skip next ch-4 sp and next st; repeat from ★ around; join with slip st to first sc: 60 sts and 40 ch-5 sps.

Rnd 11: Slip st in next sc, ch 8, (tr, ch 3, tr) in next tr, ch 4, skip next ch-5 sp and next sc, ★ tr in next sc, ch 4, (tr, ch 3, tr) in next tr, ch 4, skip next ch-5 sp and next sc; repeat from ★ around; join with slip st to fourth ch of beginning ch-8: 60 sts and 60 sps.

Rnd 12: Slip st in next 4 chs, slip st in next tr and in next ch-3 sp, work (Beginning 3-tr Cluster, ch 3, 3-tr Cluster) in same sp, ★ † ch 4, skip next 2 ch-4 sps, tr in next ch-3 sp, (ch 2, tr in same sp) 5 times, ch 4, skip next 2 ch-4 sps †, work (3-tr Cluster, ch 3, 3-tr Cluster) in next ch-3 sp; repeat from ★ 8 times **more**, then repeat from † to † once; join with slip st to top of Beginning 3-tr Cluster: 80 sps.

Rnd 13: Slip st in first ch-3 sp, work (Beginning 3-tr Cluster, ch 3, 3-tr Cluster) in same sp, ★ † ch 5, skip next ch-4 sp, work Popcorn in next ch-2 sp, (ch 2, work Popcorn in next ch-2 sp) 4 times, ch 5, skip next ch-4 sp †, work (3-tr Cluster, ch 3, 3-tr Cluster) in next ch-3 sp; repeat from ★ 8 times **more**, then repeat from † to † once; join with slip st to top of Beginning 3-tr Cluster: 70 sts and 70 sps.

Rnd 14: Slip st in first ch-3 sp, work (Beginning 3-tr Cluster, ch 3, 3-tr Cluster) in same sp, ★ † ch 6, skip next ch-5 sp, work Popcorn in next ch-2 sp, (ch 2, work Popcorn in next ch-2 sp) 3 times, ch 6, skip next ch-5 sp †, work (3-tr Cluster, ch 3, 3-tr Cluster) in next ch-3 sp; repeat from ★ 8 times **more**, then repeat from † to † once; join with slip st to top of Beginning 3-tr Cluster: 60 sts and 60 sps.

Rnd 15: (Slip st, work Beginning 3-tr Cluster) in first ch-3 sp, ★ † (ch 3, work 3-tr Cluster in same sp) twice, ch 7, skip next ch-6 sp, work Popcorn in next ch-2 sp, (ch 2, work Popcorn in next ch-2 sp) twice, ch 7, skip next ch-6 sp †, work 3-tr Cluster in next ch-3 sp; repeat from ★ 8 times **more**, then repeat from † to † once; join with slip st to top of Beginning 3-tr Cluster.

Rnd 16: Slip st in first ch-3 sp, work (Beginning 3-tr Cluster, ch 3, 3-tr Cluster) in same sp, ★ † ch 8, slip st in fourth ch from hook (Picot made), ch 4, work (3-tr Cluster, ch 3, 3-tr Cluster) in next ch-3 sp, ch 7, skip next ch-7 sp, work Popcorn in next ch-2 sp, ch 2, work Popcorn in next ch-2 sp, ch 7, skip next ch-7 sp †, work (3-tr Cluster, ch 3, 3-tr Cluster) in next ch-3 sp; repeat from ★ 8 times **more**, then repeat from † to † once; join with slip st to top of Beginning 3-tr Cluster: 60 sts, 10 Picots, and 70 sps.

Rnd 17: Slip st in first ch-3 sp, work (Beginning 3-tr Cluster, ch 3, 3-tr Cluster) in same sp, ★ † ch 4, skip next ch-4 sp, 7 tr in next Picot (ch-4 sp), ch 4, skip next ch-4 sp, work (3-tr Cluster, ch 3, 3-tr Cluster) in next ch-3 sp, ch 7, skip next ch-7 sp, work Popcorn in next ch-2 sp, ch 7, skip next ch-7 sp †, work (3-tr Cluster, ch 3, 3-tr Cluster) in next ch-3 sp; repeat from ★ 8 times **more**, then repeat from † to † once; join with slip st to top of Beginning 3-tr Cluster: 120 sts and 60 sps.

Rnd 18: Slip st in first ch-3 sp, work (Beginning 3-tr Cluster, ch 3, 3-tr Cluster) in same sp, ★ † ch 4, skip next ch-4 sp, 2 tr in each of next 7 tr, ch 4, skip next ch-4 sp, work (3-tr Cluster, ch 3, 3-tr Cluster) in next ch-3 sp, ch 4, skip next ch-7 sp, sc in top of next Popcorn, ch 4, skip next ch-7 sp †, work (3-tr Cluster, ch 3, 3-tr Cluster) in next ch-3 sp; repeat from ★ 8 times **more**, then repeat from † to † once; join with slip st to top of Beginning 3-tr Cluster: 190 sts and 60 sps.

Rnd 19: Slip st in first ch-3 sp, work (Beginning 3-tr Cluster, ch 3, 3-tr Cluster) in same sp, ★ † ch 4, skip next ch-4 sp, tr in next tr, ch 3, (work 2-tr Cluster, ch 3) twice, 2 tr in each of next 4 tr, ch 3, (work 2-tr Cluster, ch 3) twice, tr in next tr, ch 4, skip next ch-4 sp, work (3-tr Cluster, ch 3, 3-tr Cluster) in next ch-3 sp, ch 4, skip next ch-4 sp, sc in next sc, ch 4, skip next ch-4 sp †, work (3-tr Cluster, ch 3, 3-tr Cluster) in next ch-3 sp; repeat from ★ 8 times **more**, then repeat from † to † once; join with slip st to top of Beginning 3-tr Cluster: 190 sts and 120 sps.

Rnd 20: Slip st in first ch-3 sp, work (Beginning 3-tr Cluster, ch 3, 3-tr Cluster) in same sp, ★ † ch 4, skip next ch-4 sp, tr in next tr, ch 3, (skip next ch, tr in next ch, ch 2, tr in next 2-tr Cluster, ch 3) twice, work 2-tr Cluster, ch 3, tr in next 4 tr, ch 3, work 2-tr Cluster, ch 3, tr in next 2-tr Cluster, (ch 2, skip next ch, tr in next ch, ch 3, skip next ch, tr in next st) twice, ch 4, skip next ch-4 sp, work (3-tr Cluster, ch 3, 3-tr Cluster) in next ch-3 sp, skip next 2 ch-4 sps †, work (3-tr Cluster, ch 3, 3-tr Cluster) in next ch-3 sp; repeat from ★ 8 times **more**, then repeat from † to † once; join with slip st to top of Beginning 3-tr Cluster: 200 sts and 160 sps.

Instructions continued on page 30.

Rnd 21: Slip st in next ch, ch 1, sc in same ch-3 sp, ★ † ch 4, skip next ch-4 sp, [(2 tr, work Picot, tr) in next ch-3 sp, ch 3, sc in next sp, ch 3] 3 times, skip next tr, tr in next tr, (tr, work Picot, tr) in next tr, [ch 3, sc in next sp, ch 3, (2 tr, work Picot, tr) in next ch-3 sp] 3 times, ch 4, skip next ch-4 sp, sc in next ch-3 sp, skip next 3-tr Cluster, (2 tr, work Picot, tr) in sp **before** next 3-tr Cluster *(Fig. 13, page 39)* †, sc in next ch-3 sp; repeat from ★ 8 times **more**, then repeat from † to † once; join with slip st to first sc, finish off.

See Washing and Blocking, page 39.

Design by Margaret Rost.

MAY
Instructions continued from page 10.

Rnd 12: (Slip st, ch 1, sc) in first ch-4 sp, ★ † (ch 4, sc in next ch-4 sp) 3 times, ch 2, skip next ch-1 sp, 2 dc in next ch-1 sp, (ch 1, 2 dc in same sp) twice, ch 2, skip next ch-1 sp †, sc in next ch-4 sp; repeat from ★ 6 times **more**, then repeat from † to † once; join with slip st to first sc: 80 sts and 56 sps.

Rnd 13: (Slip st, ch 1, sc) in first ch-4 sp, ★ † (ch 4, sc in next ch-4 sp) twice, ch 3, skip next ch-2 sp, [(2 dc, ch 1, 2 dc) in next ch-1 sp, ch 3] twice, skip next ch-2 sp †, sc in next ch-4 sp; repeat from ★ 6 times **more**, then repeat from † to † once; join with slip st to first sc: 56 sps.

Rnd 14: (Slip st, ch 1, sc) in first ch-4 sp, ★ † ch 4, sc in next ch-4 sp, ch 3, skip next ch-3 sp, (2 dc, ch 1, 2 dc) in next ch-1 sp, ch 5, sc in next ch-3 sp, ch 5, (2 dc, ch 1, 2 dc) in next ch-1 sp, ch 3, skip next ch-3 sp †, sc in next ch-4 sp; repeat from ★ 6 times **more**, then repeat from † to † once; join with slip st to first sc.

Rnd 15: Slip st in next 2 chs, ch 6, ★ † skip next ch-3 sp, (2 dc, ch 1, 2 dc) in next ch-1 sp, ch 5, (sc in next ch-5 sp, ch 5) twice, (2 dc, ch 1, 2 dc) in next ch-1 sp †, ch 3, skip next ch-3 sp, dc in next ch-4 sp, ch 3; repeat from ★ 6 times **more**, then repeat from † to † once, ch 2, skip last ch-3 sp, sc in third ch of beginning ch-6 to form last ch-3 sp.

Rnd 16: [Ch 2, dc in next ch-3 sp (decrease made)], ★ † (2 dc, ch 1, 2 dc) in next ch-1 sp, ch 5, (sc in next ch-5 sp, ch 5) 3 times, (2 dc, ch 1, 2 dc) in next ch-1 sp †, decrease; repeat from ★ 6 times **more**, then repeat from † to † once; join with slip st to first dc: 96 sts and 48 sps.

Rnd 17: Ch 3, (dc, ch 1, 2 dc) in same st, ★ † ch 2, sc in next ch-1 sp, (ch 5, sc in next sp) 5 times, ch 2, skip next 2 dc †, (2 dc, ch 1, 2 dc) in next dc; repeat from ★ 6 times **more**, then repeat from † to † once; join with slip st to first dc: 80 sts and 64 sps.

Rnd 18: Slip st in next dc and in next ch-1 sp, ch 1, sc in same sp, ch 5, ★ skip next ch-2 sp, (sc in next ch-5 sp, ch 5) 5 times, skip next ch-2 sp, sc in next ch-1 sp, ch 5; repeat from ★ around to last 7 sps, skip next ch-2 sp, sc in next ch-5 sp, (ch 5, sc in next ch-5 sp) 4 times, ch 2, skip last ch-2 sp, dc in first sc to form last ch-5 sp: 48 ch-5 sps.

Rnd 19: Ch 1, sc in last ch-5 sp made, (ch 6, sc in next ch-5 sp) around, ch 3, dc in first sc to form last ch-6 sp.

Rnd 20: Ch 1, sc in last ch-6 sp made, (ch 6, sc in next ch-6 sp) 3 times, 11 tr in next ch-6 sp, sc in next ch-6 sp, ★ (ch 6, sc in next ch-6 sp) 4 times, 11 tr in next ch-6 sp, sc in next ch-6 sp; repeat from ★ around, ch 3, dc in first sc to form last ch-6 sp: 128 sts and 32 ch-6 sps.

Rnd 21: Ch 1, sc in last ch-6 sp made, ★ † (ch 6, sc in next ch-6 sp) 3 times, ch 3, skip next sc, dc in next tr, (ch 1, dc in next tr) 10 times, ch 3 †, sc in next ch-6 sp; repeat from ★ 6 times **more**, then repeat from † to † once; join with slip st to first sc: 120 sts and 120 sps.

Rnd 22: Slip st in next 2 chs, ch 1, sc in same ch-6 sp, ch 6, (sc in next ch-6 sp, ch 6) twice, ★ † skip next ch-3 sp, dc in next dc, (ch 2, dc in next dc) 10 times †, ch 6, skip next ch-3 sp, (sc in next ch-6 sp, ch 6) 3 times; repeat from ★ 6 times **more**, then repeat from † to † once, ch 3, dc in first sc to form last ch-6 sp: 112 sts and 112 sps.

Rnd 23: Ch 1, sc in last ch-6 sp made, ★ † (ch 6, sc in next ch-6 sp) 3 times, ch 3, (dc in next dc, ch 3) 11 times †, sc in next ch-6 sp; repeat from ★ 6 times **more**, then repeat from † to † once; join with slip st to first sc: 120 sts and 120 sps.

Rnd 24: Slip st in next 2 chs, ch 1, sc in same ch-6 sp, ★ † (ch 6, sc in next ch-6 sp) twice, ch 3, skip next sc, (dc in next dc, ch 3) 11 times, skip next ch-3 sp †, sc in next ch-6 sp; repeat from ★ 6 times **more**, then repeat from † to † once; join with slip st to first sc: 112 sts and 112 sps.

Rnd 25: Slip st in next 2 chs, ch 1, sc in same ch-6 sp, ★ † ch 6, sc in next ch-6 sp, ch 3, skip next sc, (dc in next dc, ch 3) 11 times, skip next ch-3 sp †, sc in next ch-6 sp; repeat from ★ 6 times **more**, then repeat from † to † once; join with slip st to first sc: 104 sts and 104 sps.

Rnd 26: Slip st in next 2 chs, ch 3, (dc, ch 1, 2 dc) in same ch-6 sp, ★ † ch 5, skip next sc, (sc in next dc, ch 5) 11 times, skip next ch-3 sp †, (2 dc, ch 1, 2 dc) in next ch-6 sp; repeat from ★ 6 times **more**, then repeat from † to † once; join with slip st to first dc.

Rnd 27: Slip st in next dc and in next ch-1 sp, ch 1, (sc, ch 4, sc) in same sp, ★ † ch 5, skip next ch-5 sp, (3 dc, ch 3, 3 dc) in next 10 ch-5 sps, ch 5, skip next ch-5 sp †, (sc, ch 4, sc) in next ch-1 sp; repeat from ★ 6 times **more**, then repeat from † to † once; join with slip st to first sc.

Rnd 28: Slip st in next ch, ch 1, sc in same ch-4 sp, ch 6, ★ skip next ch-5 sp, (sc in next ch-3 sp, ch 6) 10 times, skip next ch-5 sp, sc in next ch-4 sp, ch 6; repeat from ★ around to last 12 sps, skip next ch-5 sp, sc in next ch-3 sp, (ch 6, sc in next ch-3 sp) 9 times, ch 3, skip last ch-5 sp, dc in first sc to form last ch-6 sp: 88 ch-6 sps.

Rnd 29: Ch 1, sc in last ch-6 sp made, (ch 6, sc in next ch-6 sp) around, ch 2, tr in first sc to form last ch-6 sp.

Rnd 30: Ch 1, (sc, ch 3, sc) in last ch-6 sp made, ch 6, ★ (sc, ch 3, sc) in next ch-6 sp, ch 6; repeat from ★ around; join with slip st to first sc, finish off.

See Washing and Blocking, page 39.

Design by Emma M. Willey.

JUNE
Instructions continued from page 12.

Rnd 13: Ch 1, sc in last ch-7 sp made, ★ † ch 3, slip st in next sc, ch 3, skip next 3 chs, (slip st, ch 5, slip st, ch 7, slip st, ch 5, slip st) in next ch, ch 3, slip st in next sc, ch 3 †, sc in next ch-7 sp; repeat from ★ 10 times **more**, then repeat from † to † once; join with slip st to first sc: 12 sc and 84 sps.

Rnd 14: Ch 1, sc in same st, ch 7, skip next 3 sps, sc in next ch-7 sp, ★ ch 7, skip next 3 sps, sc in next sc, ch 7, skip next 3 sps, sc in next ch-7 sp; repeat from ★ around to last 3 sps, ch 3, skip last 3 sps, tr in first sc to form last ch-7 sp: 24 ch-7 sps.

Rnd 15: Ch 1, 4 sc in last ch-7 sp made, slip st in next sc, 6 sc in next ch-7 sp, decrease, work Picot, ★ 6 sc in same sp as second half of decrease, slip st in next sc, 6 sc in next ch-7 sp, decrease, work Picot; repeat from ★ around, 2 sc in same st as second half of decrease; join with slip st to first sc: 168 sts and 12 Picots.

Rnd 16: Ch 1, sc in same st, ch 9, skip next 7 sts, sc in next sc, ★ ch 9, skip next Picot and next 2 sc, sc in next sc, ch 9, skip next 7 sts, sc in next sc; repeat from ★ around to last Picot, ch 4, skip last Picot and last 2 sc, dtr in first sc to form last ch-9 sp: 24 ch-9 sps.

Rnd 17: Ch 1, sc in last ch-9 sp made, (ch 10, sc in next ch-9 sp) around, ch 5, dtr in first sc to form last loop.

Rnd 18: Ch 1, sc in last loop made, ch 11, (sc in next loop, ch 11) around; join with slip st to first sc.

Rnd 19: Ch 5, skip next 5 chs, (slip st, ch 6, slip st, ch 8, slip st, ch 6, slip st) in next ch, ch 5, ★ slip st in next sc, ch 5, skip next 5 chs, (slip st, ch 6, slip st, ch 8, slip st, ch 6, slip st) in next ch, ch 5; repeat from ★ around; join with slip st to joining slip st: 120 sps.

Rnd 20: Ch 1, sc in same st, ch 5, ★ skip next ch-5 sp, (sc in next sp, ch 5) 3 times, skip next ch-5 sp, sc in next slip st, ch 5; repeat from ★ around to last 5 sps, skip next ch-5 sp, sc in next ch-6 sp, (ch 5, sc in next sp) twice, ch 1, tr in first sc to form last ch-5 sp: 96 ch-5 sps.

Instructions continued on page 32.

Rnd 21: Ch 1, sc in last ch-5 sp made and in next ch-5 sp, 4 sc in next ch-5 sp, decrease, work Picot, 4 sc in same sp as second half of decrease, ★ sc in next 2 ch-5 sps, 4 sc in next ch-5 sp, decrease, work Picot, 4 sc in same sp as second half of decrease; repeat from ★ around; join with slip st to first sc: 264 sts and 24 Picots.

Rnd 22: Slip st in next 4 sc, ch 1, sc in same st, ch 9, skip next Picot and next sc, sc in next sc, ch 9, skip next 6 sc, ★ sc in next sc, ch 9, skip next Picot and next sc, sc in next sc, ch 9, skip next 6 sc; repeat from ★ around; join with slip st to first sc: 48 ch-9 sps.

Rnd 23: Ch 1, sc in same st, ch 4, skip next 4 chs, (slip st, ch 6, slip st, ch 8, slip st, ch 6, slip st) in next ch, ch 4, ★ sc in next sc, ch 4, skip next 4 chs, (slip st, ch 6, slip st, ch 8, slip st, ch 6, slip st) in next ch, ch 4; repeat from ★ around; join with slip st to first sc: 240 sps.

Rnd 24: Ch 1, sc in same st, ch 5, ★ skip next ch-4 sp, (sc in next sp, ch 5) 3 times, skip next ch-4 sp, sc in next sc, ch 5; repeat from ★ around to last 5 sps, skip next ch-4 sp, sc in next ch-6 sp, (ch 5, sc in next sp) twice, ch 1, tr in first sc to form last ch-5 sp: 192 ch-5 sps.

Rnd 25: Ch 1, sc in last ch-5 sp made and in next ch-5 sp, 4 sc in next ch-5 sp, decrease, work Picot, 4 sc in same sp as second half of decrease, ★ sc in next 2 ch-5 sps, 4 sc in next ch-5 sp, decrease, work Picot, 4 sc in same sp as second half of decrease; repeat from ★ around; join with slip st to first sc, finish off.

See Washing and Blocking, page 39.

Design by Ocie Jordan.

Rnd 10: Ch 1, sc in same st, ★ † ch 2, (2 dtr, ch 2) 5 times in next ch-5 sp, skip next 6 sc, sc in next sc, ch 2, (2 tr, ch 2) 4 times in next ch-3 sp, skip next 5 sc †, sc in next sc; repeat from ★ 4 times **more**, then repeat from † to † once; join with slip st to first sc: 120 sts and 66 ch-2 sps.

Rnd 11: Slip st in next 2 chs and in next dtr, ch 1, sc in same st and in next dtr, ★ † [(sc, ch 3, sc) in next ch-2 sp, sc in next 2 dtr] 4 times, skip next 2 ch-2 sps, sc in next 2 tr, [(sc, ch 3, sc) in next ch-2 sp, sc in next 2 tr] 3 times, skip next 2 ch-2 sps †, sc in next 2 dtr; repeat from ★ 4 times **more**, then repeat from † to † once; join with slip st to first sc: 42 ch-3 sps.

Rnd 12: Slip st in next 2 sc and in next ch-3 sp, ch 1, 3 sc in same sp, ★ † (ch 4, 3 sc in next ch-3 sp) 3 times, ch 1, 3 sc in next ch-3 sp, (ch 4, 3 sc in next ch-3 sp) twice, ch 1 †, 3 sc in next ch-3 sp; repeat from ★ 4 times **more**, then repeat from † to † once; join with slip st to first sc: 126 sc and 42 sps.

Rnd 13: Ch 1, sc in same st and in next 2 sc, ★ † [(sc, 2 dc, work Picot, dc, sc) in next ch-4 sp, sc in next 3 sc] 3 times, skip next ch, sc in next 3 sc, [(sc, 2 dc, work Picot, dc, sc) in next ch-4 sp, sc in next 3 sc] twice, skip next ch †, sc in next 3 sc; repeat from ★ 4 times **more**, then repeat from † to † once; join with slip st to first sc, finish off: 30 Picots.

Rnd 14: With **right** side facing, join Blue with sc in first Picot; ch 10, (sc in next Picot, ch 10) around; join with slip st to first sc: 30 loops.

Rnd 15: Ch 1, sc in same st, (5 sc, ch 3, 5 sc) in next loop, ★ sc in next sc, (5 sc, ch 3, 5 sc) in next loop; repeat from ★ around; join with slip st to first sc: 330 sc and 30 ch-3 sps.

Rnd 16: Ch 1, sc in same st, ch 2, (2 tr, ch 2) 3 times in next ch-3 sp, skip next 5 sc, ★ sc in next sc, ch 2, (2 tr, ch 2) 3 times in next ch-3 sp, skip next 5 sc; repeat from ★ around; join with slip st to first sc: 210 sts and 120 ch-2 sps.

Rnd 17: Slip st in next 2 chs and in next tr, ch 1, sc in same st and in next tr, ★ † [(sc, ch 3, sc) in next ch-2 sp, sc in next 2 tr] twice, skip next 2 ch-2 sps †, sc in next 2 tr; repeat from ★ 28 times **more**, then repeat from † to † once; join with slip st to first sc: 300 sc and 60 ch-3 sps.

Rnd 18: Slip st in next sc, ch 1, sc in same st and in next sc, ★ † 3 sc in next ch-3 sp, ch 6, slip st in fourth ch from hook, ch 2, 3 sc in next ch-3 sp, sc in next 2 sc, skip next 2 sc †, sc in next 2 sc; repeat from ★ 28 times **more**, then repeat from † to † once; join with slip st to first sc, finish off.

See Washing and Blocking, page 39.

Design by Patricia Kristoffersen.

AUGUST
Instructions continued from page 16.

Rnd 13: Skip next 2 hdc, work Shell in next hdc, skip next 2 hdc, ★ slip st in next hdc, skip next 2 hdc, work Shell in next hdc, skip next 2 hdc; repeat from ★ around; join with slip st to joining slip st: 320 sts.

Rnd 14: Slip st in next 5 sts, ch 9, skip next 9 sts, ★ slip st in next tr, ch 9, skip next 9 sts; repeat from ★ around; join with slip st to slip st at base of first ch-9: 32 ch-9 sps.

Rnd 15: Ch 1, 11 sc in each ch-9 sp around; join with slip st to first sc: 352 sc.

Rnd 16: Ch 1, sc in same st and in next 4 sc, (slip st, ch 3, work Popcorn, ch 3, slip st) in next sc, ★ sc in next 10 sc, (slip st, ch 3, work Popcorn, ch 3, slip st) in next sc; repeat from ★ around to last 5 sc, sc in last 5 sc; join with slip st to first sc: 320 sc and 32 Popcorns.

Rnd 17: Ch 1, sc in same st and in next 2 sc, ch 11, ★ skip next Popcorn and next 2 sc, sc in next 6 sc, ch 11; repeat from ★ around to last Popcorn, skip last Popcorn and next 2 sc, sc in last 3 sc; join with slip st to first sc: 32 loops.

Rnd 18: Slip st in next 2 sc, ch 1, 17 hdc in each loop around; join with slip st to first hdc, finish off.

TRIM
Rnd 1: With **right** side facing, working in **front** of previous rnds and in slip sts between Shells on Rnd 13, join White with slip st in any slip st; work Beginning Popcorn in same st, ch 9, skip next Shell, ★ work Popcorn in next slip st, ch 9, skip next Shell; repeat from ★ around; join with slip st to top of Beginning Popcorn: 32 ch-9 sps.

Rnd 2: Ch 1, 11 hdc in each ch-9 sp around; join with slip st to first hdc, finish off.

FLOWER
With White, ch 8; join with slip st to form a ring.

Rnd 1 (Right side)**:** Ch 1, 16 sc in ring; join with slip st to first sc.

Note: Mark Rnd 1 as **right** side.

Rnd 2: Work Beginning Popcorn in same st, work Popcorn in next sc, ch 5, (work Popcorn in next 2 sc, ch 5) around; join with slip st to top of Beginning Popcorn, finish off: 8 ch-5 sps.

Rnd 3: With **right** side facing, join Lt Blue with slip st in any ch-5 sp; ch 2 (**counts as first hdc**), 10 hdc in same sp, 11 hdc in each ch-5 sp around; join with slip st to first hdc, finish off.

With matching thread, sew Flower to Rnd 1 of Doily.

See Washing and Blocking, page 39.

Design by Josie Rabier.

SEPTEMBER
Instructions continued from page 18.

Rnd 19: Ch 3, 2 dc in last ch-3 sp made, ★ † ch 2, skip next ch-1 sp, sc in next ch-4 sp, (ch 4, sc in next ch-4 sp) 6 times, ch 2, skip next ch-1 sp †, (3 dc, ch 3, 3 dc) in next ch-3 sp; repeat from ★ 6 times **more**, then repeat from † to † once, 3 dc in same sp as first dc, ch 1, hdc in first dc to form last ch-3 sp: 72 sps.

Rnd 20: Ch 3, (2 dc, ch 3, 3 dc) in last ch-3 sp made, ch 3, ★ † skip next ch-2 sp, sc in next ch-4 sp, (ch 4, sc in next ch-4 sp) 5 times, ch 3, skip next ch-2 sp †, (3 dc, ch 3) 3 times in next ch-3 sp; repeat from ★ 6 times **more**, then repeat from † to † once, 3 dc in same sp as first dc, ch 1, hdc in first dc to form last ch-3 sp.

Rnd 21: Ch 3, 2 dc in last ch-3 sp made, ★ † ch 5, (3 dc, ch 3) twice in next ch-3 sp, skip next ch-3 sp, sc in next ch-4 sp, (ch 4, sc in next ch-4 sp) 4 times, ch 3, skip next ch-3 sp †, (3 dc, ch 3, 3 dc) in next ch-3 sp; repeat from ★ 6 times **more**, then repeat from † to † once, 3 dc in same sp as first dc, ch 1, hdc in first dc to form last ch-3 sp.

Rnd 22: Ch 3, 2 dc in last ch-3 sp made, ★ † ch 7, skip next ch-5 sp, (3 dc, ch 3) twice in next ch-3 sp, skip next ch-3 sp, sc in next ch-4 sp, (ch 4, sc in next ch-4 sp) 3 times, ch 3, skip next ch-3 sp †, (3 dc, ch 3, 3 dc) in next ch-3 sp; repeat from ★ 6 times **more**, then repeat from † to † once, 3 dc in same sp as first dc, ch 1, hdc in first dc to form last ch-3 sp: 64 sps.

Rnd 23: Ch 3, 2 dc in last ch-3 sp made, ★ † ch 5, working **around** next ch-7, sc in next ch-5 sp on Rnd 21, ch 5, (3 dc, ch 3) twice in next ch-3 sp, skip next ch-3 sp, sc in next ch-4 sp, (ch 4, sc in next ch-4 sp) twice, ch 3, skip next ch-3 sp †, (3 dc, ch 3, 3 dc) in next ch-3 sp; repeat from ★ 6 times **more**, then repeat from † to † once, 3 dc in same sp as first dc, ch 1, hdc in first dc to form last ch-3 sp.

Rnd 24: Ch 3, 2 dc in last ch-3 sp made, ★ † ch 5, sc in next ch-5 sp, sc in next sc and in next ch-5 sp, ch 5, (3 dc, ch 3) twice in next ch-3 sp, skip next ch-3 sp, sc in next ch-4 sp, ch 4, sc in next ch-4 sp, ch 3, skip next ch-3 sp †, (3 dc, ch 3, 3 dc) in next ch-3 sp; repeat from ★ 6 times **more**, then repeat from † to † once, 3 dc in same sp as first dc, ch 1, hdc in first dc to form last ch-3 sp: 40 sc and 56 sps.

Rnd 25: Ch 3, 2 dc in last ch-3 sp made, ★ † ch 6, sc in next ch-5 sp, sc in next 3 sc and in next ch-5 sp, ch 6, (3 dc, ch 3) twice in next ch-3 sp, skip next ch-3 sp, sc in next ch-4 sp, ch 3, skip next ch-3 sp †, (3 dc, ch 3, 3 dc) in next ch-3 sp; repeat from ★ 6 times **more**, then repeat from † to † once, 3 dc in same sp as first dc, ch 1, hdc in first dc to form last ch-3 sp: 48 sc and 48 sps.

Rnd 26: Ch 3, 2 dc in last ch-3 sp made, ★ † ch 7, 2 sc in next ch-6 sp, sc in next 5 sc, 2 sc in next ch-6 sp, ch 7, (3 dc, ch 3, 3 dc) in next ch-3 sp, ch 4, skip next ch-3 sp, sc in next sc, ch 4, skip next ch-3 sp †, (3 dc, ch 3, 3 dc) in next ch-3 sp; repeat from ★ 6 times **more**, then repeat from † to † once, 3 dc in same sp as first dc, ch 1, hdc in first dc to form last ch-3 sp: 80 sc and 48 sps.

Rnd 27: Ch 3, 2 dc in last ch-3 sp made, ★ † ch 8, 3 sc in next ch-7 sp, sc in next 9 sc, 3 sc in next ch-7 sp, ch 8, (3 dc, ch 3, 3 dc) in next ch-3 sp, skip next 2 ch-4 sps †, (3 dc, ch 3, 3 dc) in next ch-3 sp; repeat from ★ 6 times **more**, then repeat from † to † once, 3 dc in same sp as first dc, ch 1, hdc in first dc to form last ch-3 sp: 120 sc and 32 sps.

Rnd 28: Ch 3, (dc, ch 2, sc) in last ch-3 sp made, ★ † sc in next 3 dc, 9 sc in next ch-8 sp, sc in next 15 sc, 9 sc in next ch-8 sp, sc in next 3 dc, (sc, ch 2, 2 dc, ch 3, 3 dc) in next ch-3 sp †, (3 dc, ch 3, 2 dc, ch 2, sc) in next ch-3 sp; repeat from ★ 6 times **more**, then repeat from † to † once, 3 dc in same sp as first dc, ch 1, hdc in first dc to form last ch-3 sp: 408 sts and 32 sps.

Rnd 29: Ch 1, 2 sc in last ch-3 sp made, sc in each st and in each ch across to next ch-3 sp, 2 sc in next ch-3 sp, ch 5, sc in fifth ch from hook, ★ 2 sc in next ch-3 sp, sc in each st and in each ch across to next ch-3 sp, 2 sc in next ch-3 sp, ch 5, sc in fifth ch from hook; repeat from ★ around; join with slip st to first sc, finish off.

See Washing and Blocking, page 39.

Design by Ocie Jordan.

34

Rnd 10: Ch 1, sc in last ch-5 sp made, ch 5, work Popcorn in center ch of next ch-5, ch 5, ★ (sc in next ch-5 sp, ch 5) twice, work Popcorn in center ch of next ch-5, ch 5; repeat from ★ around to last ch-5 sp, sc in last ch-5 sp, ch 2, dc in first sc to form last ch-5 sp.

Rnd 11: Ch 5, dtr in top of last dc made, ch 3, (2 dtr in center ch of next ch-5, ch 3) around; join with slip st to first dtr: 96 dtr and 48 ch-3 sps.

Rnd 12: Ch 1, sc in same st and in next dtr, 3 sc in next ch-3 sp, (sc in next 2 dtr, 3 sc in next ch-3 sp) around; join with slip st to first sc: 240 sc.

Rnd 13: Ch 5, dtr in next sc, ch 3, skip next 3 sc, ★ dtr in next 2 sc, ch 3, skip next 3 sc; repeat from ★ around; join with slip st to first dtr: 96 dtr and 48 ch-3 sps.

Rnd 14: Ch 1, sc in same st and in next dtr, 3 sc in next ch-3 sp, (sc in next 2 dtr, 3 sc in next ch-3 sp) around; join with slip st to first sc: 240 sc.

Rnd 15: Ch 5, dtr in next sc, ch 4, skip next 3 sc, ★ dtr in next 2 sc, ch 4, skip next 3 sc; repeat from ★ around; join with slip st to first dtr: 96 dtr and 48 ch-4 sps.

Rnd 16: Ch 1, sc in same st and in next dtr, 5 sc in next ch-4 sp, (sc in next 2 dtr, 5 sc in next ch-4 sp) around; join with slip st to Back Loop Only of first sc: 336 sc.

Rnd 17: Ch 1, sc in Back Loop Only of same st and each sc around; join with slip st to **both** loops of first sc.

Rnd 18: Ch 1, sc in same st, ★ ch 5, skip next 3 sc, sc in next sc; repeat from ★ around to last 3 sc, ch 2, skip last 3 sc, dc in first sc to form last ch-5 sp: 84 ch-5 sps.

Rnd 19: Work Beginning Popcorn in top of last dc made, ★ † (ch 2, work Popcorn in center ch of next ch-5) 4 times, ch 5, (sc, ch 3, sc) in center ch of next ch-5, ch 5 †, work Popcorn in center ch of next ch-5; repeat from ★ 12 times **more**, then repeat from † to † once; join with slip st to top of Beginning Popcorn: 70 Popcorns and 98 sps.

Rnd 20: (Slip st, work Beginning Popcorn) in first ch-2 sp, ★ † (ch 2, work Popcorn in next ch-2 sp) 3 times, ch 5, [(sc, ch 3, sc) in center ch of next ch-5, ch 5] twice †, work Popcorn in next ch-2 sp; repeat from ★ 12 times **more**, then repeat from † to † once; join with slip st to top of Beginning Popcorn: 56 Popcorns and 112 sps.

Rnd 21: (Slip st, work Beginning Popcorn) in first ch-2 sp, ★ † (ch 2, work Popcorn in next ch-2 sp) twice, ch 5, [(sc, ch 3, sc) in center ch of next ch-5, ch 5] 3 times †, work Popcorn in next ch-2 sp; repeat from ★ 12 times **more**, then repeat from † to † once; join with slip st to top of Beginning Popcorn: 42 Popcorns and 126 sps.

Rnd 22: (Slip st, work Beginning Popcorn) in first ch-2 sp, ★ † ch 2, work Popcorn in next ch-2 sp, ch 5, [(sc, ch 3, sc) in center ch of next ch-5, ch 5] 4 times †, work Popcorn in next ch-2 sp; repeat from ★ 12 times **more**, then repeat from † to † once; join with slip st to top of Beginning Popcorn: 28 Popcorns and 140 sps.

Rnd 23: (Slip st, work Beginning Popcorn) in first ch-2 sp, ★ † ch 7, sc in seventh ch from hook, ch 7, sc in fifth ch from hook, ch 2, [(sc, ch 3, sc) in center ch of next ch-5, ch 7, sc in fifth ch from hook, ch 2] 5 times †, work Popcorn in next ch-2 sp; repeat from ★ 12 times **more**, then repeat from † to † once; join with slip st to top of Beginning Popcorn, finish off.

See Washing and Blocking, page 39.

Design by Ocie Jordan.

NOVEMBER
Instructions continued from page 22.

Row 45: Work Beginning Block Decrease, work Block, work 13 Spaces, work Block, leave remaining dc unworked: 2 Blocks and 13 Spaces.

Rows 46-51: Follow chart, page 22; at end of Row 51, finish off.

SHORT END
Row 1: With **wrong** side facing and working in sps and in free loops of ch across beginning ch **(Fig 4)**, join thread with dc in ch at base of marked dc **(see Joining With Dc, page 39)**; 2 dc in next sp, dc in next ch (at base of dc), (ch 2, skip next 2 chs, dc in next ch)13 times, 2 dc in next sp, dc in next ch, leave remaining chs unworked: 2 Blocks and 13 Spaces.

Fig. 4

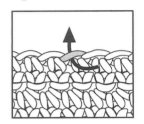

Rows 2-7: Follow Rows 46-51 of chart, page 22; at end of Row 7, finish off.

TRIM
FIRST SIDE
With **right** side facing, join thread with slip st in last dc on Row 45; (3 dc, ch 2, 3 dc) in next corner sp; working in end of rows, dc in top of next row, (2 dc in end of same row, dc in top of next row) across to Row 1, (3 dc, ch 2, 3 dc) in Row 1; join with slip st to first dc on Row 1 of Short End, finish off: 139 dc and 2 ch-2 sps.

SECOND SIDE
With **right** side facing, join thread with slip st in first dc on Row 1 of Short End; (3 dc, ch 2, 3 dc) in next corner sp; working in end of rows, dc in top of same row, (2 dc in end of next row, dc in top of same row) across to Row 44, (3 dc, ch 2, 3 dc) in Row 44; join with slip st to first dc on Row 45, do **not** finish off: 139 dc and 2 ch-2 sps.

EDGING
Rnd 1: Ch 1, sc in same st, † ch 5, (sc in first dc on next row, ch 5) 6 times, (skip next 2 dc, sc in next dc, ch 5) 3 times, (sc in last dc on next row, ch 5) 5 times, skip next 2 dc on next row, sc in same dc as slip st on Trim, ch 5, sc in next ch-2 sp, ch 5, skip next 3 dc, (sc in next dc, ch 5, skip next 4 dc) across to next ch-2 sp, sc in ch-2 sp †, ch 5, skip next 3 dc, sc in same dc as slip st on Trim, repeat from † to † once, ch 2, skip last 3 dc, dc in first sc to form last ch-5 sp: 88 ch-5 sps.

Rnd 2: Ch 4 **(counts as first dc plus ch 1, now and throughout)**, dc in last ch-5 sp made, ch 2, 5 sc in next ch-5 sp, ch 2, ★ (dc, ch 1, dc) in next ch-5 sp, ch 2, 5 sc in next ch-5 sp, ch 2; repeat from ★ around; join with slip st to first dc: 308 sts and 132 sps.

Rnd 3: (Slip st, ch 4, dc) in first ch-1 sp, ch 3, skip next ch-2 sp and next sc, sc in next 4 sc, ch 3, skip next ch-2 sp, ★ (dc, ch 1, dc) in next ch-1 sp, ch 3, skip next ch-2 sp and next sc, sc in next 4 sc, ch 3, skip next ch-2 sp; repeat from ★ around; join with slip st to first dc: 264 sts and 132 sps.

Rnd 4: (Slip st, ch 4, dc) in first ch-1 sp, ch 4, skip next ch-3 sp and next sc, sc in next 3 sc, ch 4, skip next ch-3 sp, ★ (dc, ch 1, dc) in next ch-1 sp, ch 4, skip next ch-3 sp and next sc, sc in next 3 sc, ch 4, skip next ch-3 sp; repeat from ★ around; join with slip st to first dc: 220 sts and 132 sps.

Rnd 5: (Slip st, ch 4, dc) in first ch-1 sp, ch 5, skip next ch-4 sp and next sc, sc in next 2 sc, ch 5, skip next ch-4 sp, ★ (dc, ch 1, dc) in next ch-1 sp, ch 5, skip next ch-4 sp and next sc, sc in next 2 sc, ch 5, skip next ch-4 sp; repeat from ★ around; join with slip st to first dc: 176 sts and 132 sps.

Rnd 6: (Slip st, ch 4, dc) in first ch-1 sp, ch 6, skip next ch-5 sp and next sc, sc in next sc, ch 6, skip next ch-5 sp, ★ (dc, ch 1, dc) in next ch-1 sp, ch 6, skip next ch-5 sp and next sc, sc in next sc, ch 6, skip next ch-5 sp; repeat from ★ around; join with slip st to first dc: 132 sts and 132 sps.

Rnd 7: (Slip st, ch 4, dc) in first ch-1 sp, ch 7, skip next ch-6 sp, sc in next sc, ch 7, skip next ch-6 sp, ★ (dc, ch 1, dc) in next ch-1 sp, ch 7, sc in next sc, ch 7, skip next ch-6 sp; repeat from ★ around; join with slip st to first dc, finish off.

See Washing and Blocking, page 39.

Design by Darlene Polachic.

GENERAL INSTRUCTIONS

ABBREVIATIONS

ch(s)	chain(s)
cm	centimeters
dc	double crochet(s)
dtr	double treble crochet(s)
FPdc	Front Post double crochet(s)
FPsc	Front Post single crochet(s)
FPtr	Front Post treble crochet(s)
hdc	half double crochet(s)
mm	millimeters
Rnd(s)	Round(s)
sc	single crochet(s)
sp(s)	space(s)
st(s)	stitch(es)
tr	treble crochet(s)
YO	yarn over

★ — work instructions following ★ as many **more** times as indicated in addition to the first time.

† to † — work all instructions from first † to second † **as many** times as specified.

( ) or [ ] — work enclosed instructions **as many** times as specified by the number immediately following **or** work all enclosed instructions in the stitch or space indicated **or** contains explanatory remarks.

colon (:) — the number(s) given after a colon at the end of a row or round denote(s) the number of stitches or spaces you should have on that row or round.

GAUGE

Exact gauge is **essential** for proper size. Before beginning your project, make the sample swatch given in the individual instructions in the thread and hook specified. After completing the swatch, measure it, counting your stitches and rounds carefully. If your swatch is larger or smaller than specified, **make another, changing hook size to get the correct gauge**. Keep trying until you find the size hook that will give you the specified gauge.

THREAD

The photographed items were made using bedspread weight cotton thread (size 10). Any of the following brands may be used with good results:

Aunt Lydia's® Classic Crochet
Coats Opera 10
DMC® Baroque
DMC® Cébélia
DMC® Cordonnet Special
DMC® Traditions
Grandma's Best
J. & P. Coats® Knit-Cro-Sheen®
South Maid®
Lily® Antique

CROCHET TERMINOLOGY	
UNITED STATES	**INTERNATIONAL**
slip stitch (slip st) =	single crochet (sc)
single crochet (sc) =	double crochet (dc)
half double crochet (hdc) =	half treble crochet (htr)
double crochet (dc) =	treble crochet (tr)
treble crochet (tr) =	double treble crochet (dtr)
double treble crochet (dtr) =	triple treble crochet (ttr)
skip =	miss

STEEL CROCHET HOOKS																
US	00	0	1	2	3	4	5	6	7	8	9	10	11	12	13	14
Metric - mm	3.5	3.25	2.75	2.25	2.1	2	1.9	1.8	1.65	1.5	1.4	1.3	1.1	1	.85	.75

◼◻◻◻ BEGINNER	Projects for first-time crocheters using basic stitches. Minimal shaping.
◼◼◻◻ EASY	Projects using yarn with basic stitches, repetitive stitch patterns, simple color changes, and simple shaping and finishing.
◼◼◼◻ INTERMEDIATE	Projects using a variety of techniques, such as basic lace patterns or color patterns, mid-level shaping and finishing.
◼◼◼◼ EXPERIENCED	Projects with intricate stitch patterns, techniques and dimension, such as non-repeating patterns, multi-color techniques, fine threads, small hooks, detailed shaping and refined finishing.

CHAIN

To work a chain stitch, begin with a slip knot on the hook. Bring the thread **over** hook from back to front, catching the thread with the hook and turning the hook slightly toward you to keep the thread from slipping off. Draw the thread through the slip knot **(Fig. 5) (first chain st made, *abbreviated ch*)**.

Fig. 5

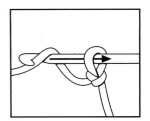

WORKING INTO THE CHAIN

Method 1: Insert hook into back ridge of each chain **(Fig. 6a)**.

Method 2: Insert hook under top two strands of each chain **(Fig. 6b)**.

Fig. 6a   **Fig. 6b**

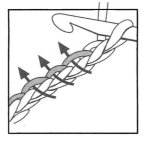 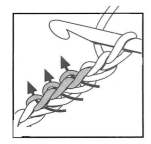

SLIP STITCH

To work a slip stitch, insert hook in stitch or space indicated, YO and draw through stitch or space and through loop on hook **(Fig. 7) (slip stitch made, *abbreviated slip st)***.

Fig. 7

SINGLE CROCHET

Insert hook in stitch or space indicated, YO and pull up a loop, YO and draw through both loops on hook **(Fig. 8) (single crochet made, *abbreviated sc)***.

Fig. 8

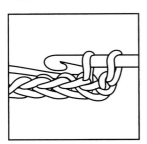

HALF DOUBLE CROCHET

YO, insert hook in stitch or space indicated, YO and pull up a loop, YO and draw through all 3 loops on hook **(Fig. 9) (half double crochet made, *abbreviated hdc)***.

Fig. 9

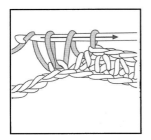

DOUBLE CROCHET

YO, insert hook in stitch or space indicated, YO and pull up a loop (3 loops on hook), YO and draw through 2 loops on hook **(Fig. 10a)**, YO and draw through remaining 2 loops on hook **(Fig. 10b) (double crochet made, *abbreviated dc)***.

Fig. 10a   **Fig. 10b**

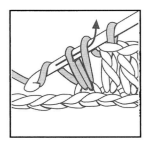 

TREBLE CROCHET

YO twice, insert hook in stitch or space indicated, YO and pull up a loop (4 loops on hook) *(Fig. 11a)*, (YO and draw through 2 loops on hook) 3 times *(Fig. 11b)* **(treble crochet made, *abbreviated tr*)**.

Fig. 11a

Fig. 11b

DOUBLE TREBLE CROCHET

YO 3 times, insert hook in stitch or space indicated, YO and pull up a loop (5 loops on hook) *(Fig. 12a)*, (YO and draw through 2 loops on hook) 4 times *(Fig. 12b)* **(treble crochet made, *abbreviated dtr*)**.

Fig. 12a

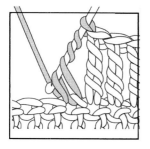

Fig. 12b

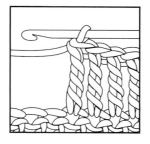

JOINING WITH SC

When instructed to join with sc, begin with a slip knot on hook. Insert hook in stitch or space indicated, YO and pull up a loop, YO and draw through both loops on hook.

JOINING WITH DC

When instructed to join with dc, begin with a slip knot on hook. YO, holding loop on hook, insert hook in stitch or space indicated, YO and pull up a loop (3 loops on hook), (YO and draw through 2 loops on hook) twice.

WORKING IN SPACE BEFORE A STITCH

When instructed to work in space **before** a stitch or in spaces **between** stitches, insert hook in space indicated by arrow *(Fig. 13)*.

Fig. 13

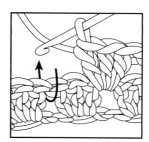

WORKING IN TOP OF A STITCH

When instructed to work in top of a stitch, work in loops indicated by arrow *(Fig 14a or 14b)*.

Fig. 14a

Fig. 14b

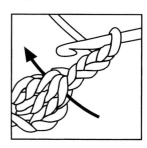

WASHING AND BLOCKING

For a more professional look, pieces should be washed and blocked. Using a mild detergent and warm water and being careful not to rub, twist, or wring, gently squeeze suds through the piece. Rinse several times in cool, clear water. Roll piece in a clean terry towel and gently press out the excess moisture. Lay piece on a flat surface and shape to proper size; where needed, pin in place using rust-proof pins. Allow to dry **completely**.

THREAD INFORMATION

Each Doily in this leaflet was made using bedspread weight cotton thread, size 10. Any brand of bedspread weight cotton thread may be used. Remember, to arrive at the finished size, it is not the brand of thread that matters, but the GAUGE/TENSION this is important.

JANUARY
DMC® Cébélia
   White (Blanc)

FEBRUARY
J. & P. Coats® Knit-Cro-Sheen®
   #1 White

MARCH
DMC® Cébélia
   #955 Lt Nile Green

APRIL
Coats Opera
   #519 Wood Violet

MAY
South Maid®
   #143 Soft Yellow

JUNE
South Maid®
   #1 White

JULY
Aunt Lydia's® Classic Crochet
   White - #1 White
   Red - #494 Victory Red
   Blue - #487 Dark Royal

AUGUST
DMC® Traditions
   White - #1 White
   Blue - #799 Med Delft Blue
   Lt Blue - #800 Pale Delft Blue

SEPTEMBER
Aunt Lydia's® Classic Crochet
   #492 Burgundy

OCTOBER
Aunt Lydia's® Classic Crochet
   #12 Black

NOVEMBER
DMC® Cébélia
   #619 Very Lt Brown

DECEMBER
DMC® Cébélia
   Blue - #799 Med Delft Blue
   Lt Blue - #800 Pale Delft Blue

We have made every effort to ensure that these instructions are accurate and complete.
We cannot, however, be responsible for human error, typographical mistakes, or variations in individual work.

Production Team: Instructional Editor - Susan Ackerman Carter; Technical Editor - Lois J. Long; Editorial Writer - Steve Cooper
Graphic Artist - Laura Atkins; Senior Graphic Artist - Rebecca J. Hester; and Photo Stylist - Sondra Daniel.

Doilies made and instructions tested by Belinda Baxter, Marianna Crowder, Vicki Kellogg, Kay Meadors, and Mary Valen.